## Praise for *Mindfulness For the Wandering Mind*

Pandit has a modern take on understanding our mind and the need for mindfulness in the connected and constantly evolving world we live in. Pandit clears up the many misconceptions surrounding mindfulness, including basics like posture. Pandit explains difficult concepts with very easy-to-understand examples, while pointing out the benefits in your everyday life that can be realized from day 1 of reading the book. I highly recommend this book to leaders of the future who are looking to lead with humility, become active listeners, and create a culture of mindfulness at the workplace.

**D. Sharma** *Founder and CEO, meditation.live*

The leadership concepts in this book challenge the way we think about our approach to leading people and the development of the leader we want to be. Anyone who is in a leadership role or is responsible for leadership development should make this book a must-read. Every page has invaluable insights to meaningful leadership. *Mindfulness and Mental Health* is a useful tool that every leader can benefit from and apply. It's honest, authentic, and engaging leadership.

**Roger Jans** *Manager of Workforce Planning Organizational Development and Classification, Ramapo College, New Jersey*

For me personally, working in banking and finance and leading international teams in a fast-paced, high-stress environment, I need all the tools I can get to remain present, empathetic, and productive. Pandit's book provides the very tools that are required to stay centered and maintain the work–life balance required for healthy living. I could not have read it at a better time.

**John Thurlow** *Chief Operating Officer, Capital Markets Division, Royal Bank of Canada*

Pandit Dasa has provided a wonderful formula for those aspiring to high levels of professional success while maintaining their personal character. As a professor at the University of Pittsburgh, I train students to be industry's leading engineers, to work efficiently with industry leaders, and to be ideal team players. I also train premed students, who are the future healthcare professionals. This book will provide the crucial tools students and professionals need to become caring and mindful professionals in the engineering and medical fields. In fact, there isn't an industry that won't benefit from this well-thought-out and highly relevant content.

**Dr. Zhi-Hong Mao** *Professor, Department of Electrical and Computer Engineering, Swanson School of Engineering, University of Pittsburgh*

I am managing teams of graduate students who are working on various research projects. Self-awareness, managing one's emotions, and peace of mind are critical for obtaining results in research. For the corporate world that will employ these students, these notions are even more important. Pandit Dasa brings his extensive corporate experience speaking about these concepts into a book. This book is a must-read for individuals looking to balance career success and personal growth. The message the book transmits – do not get lost in nonessential things – is extremely important in corporate America, an extremely competitive and hardworking environment.

**Ionut Florescu** *Research Professor in Financial Engineering, Director of Hanlon Laboratories, Director of the Financial Analytics program, School of Business, Stevens Institute of Technology*

As someone who has been in high-level sales for over 15 years, managing teams in a fast-paced, results-oriented environment, I know that it's crucial to stay focused on the goals, yet calm and present while engaging with clients. *Mindfulness and Mental Health* by Pandit Dasa provides very relevant insights on how to do exactly that. His practical tips have helped me manage my time and teams with efficiency, a clear mind, and emotional intelligence. This is a must-read for anyone aspiring to remain mindful while overseeing teams and remaining productive.

**Tushar Bajaj** *Sales Leader of Hybrid Cloud Integration, IBM North America*

# MINDFULNESS FOR THE WANDERING MIND

PANDIT DASA

# MINDFULNESS FOR THE WANDERING MIND

## LIFE-CHANGING TOOLS for MANAGING STRESS and IMPROVING MENTAL HEALTH AT WORK AND IN LIFE

WILEY

Published by John Wiley & Sons, Inc., Hoboken, New Jersey.
Published simultaneously in Canada.



For general information on our other products and services or for technical support, please contact our Customer Care Department within the United States at (800) 762-2974, outside the United States at (317) 572-3993 or fax (317) 572-4002.

Wiley also publishes its books in a variety of electronic formats. Some content that appears in print may not be available in electronic formats. For more information about Wiley products, visit our web site at www.wiley.com.

***Library of Congress Cataloging-in-Publication Data is Available:***

ISBN 9781394197620 (Cloth)
ISBN 9781394197637 (ePub)
ISBN 9781394197644 (ePDF)

Cover Design: Chris Wallace
Cover Images: © sensationaldesign/Getty Images, © Art-Digital-Illustration/Getty Images
Author Photo: Courtesy of the Author

SKY10049250_061623

# Contents

# Foreword

*Mindfulness and Mental Health* offers wisdom with immediate practical applications and a process of focused, integrating *questions* to help you guide yourself, your colleagues, direct reports, and teams forward in a mindful way. Pandit works from the idea of servant leadership and the practice of focusing the mind to help develop the ability to be resilient, tune up responsiveness to conflict, and achieve stronger professional relationships.

Before moving into his career as an educator in leadership, Pandit Dasa spent 15 years as a monk, living in a small urban monastery located in the East Village in New York City. He slept on a two-inch-thick and two-foot-wide sleeping mat, upgrading in his final three years to a bed with a sleeping bag. As Dasa describes in his first book, *Urban Monk*: "Our monastery is a six-story brownstone on the same block as several nightclubs and bars, a tattoo shop, a funeral home, and a drag queen cabaret."

In this big-city environment, Pandit practiced and learned. He shares his transformational leadership insights in *Mindfulness and Mental Health*. The purpose of this book is to help readers "manage the vehicle of the mind." It might seem surprising that his former training facility, the monastery, wasn't located on an isolated mountaintop, far removed from the marketplaces of civilization. Instead, the monastery where Pandit gained the knowledge he shares in this book was established right in the kind of environment where we all must perform: a noisy, hectic landscape of competing, complex interests. Your office might be in any city in the world and it likely won't be in a location more intense and distracting than New York City. As I write this Foreword, it is the month of April. The year is 2020 and all the cities of the world are in some stage of sudden quiet, quarantined against the pandemic of COVID-19. But noisy or quiet, we work in competitive environments; noisy or quiet, the stress in our lives doesn't evaporate. Because of the pressure we confront, it is too easy for us to blame our distraction, lack of focus, and various anxieties on our external environment. Pandit reminds us: We need to get rid of the excuse "I can't meditate because my mind is too restless." That restlessness is exactly why we need to meditate. Pandit offers an encouraging approach based on his own experience. If you have tried meditation, you know the challenge of your mind wandering. Pandit walks us through his own meditation process, offering specific actions to help you succeed and make meditation a part of your toolkit. Pandit understands that for the reader to succeed, they will require patience. "There's no need to get frustrated or upset if the mind wanders off, because that's just what the mind does."

In his years at the monastery, Pandit and his fellow monks would wake to meditate at 4:00 a.m., after sweeping their floors clean. They would often hear the explosive voices of inebriated people on the streets, as well as the occasional fistfight. I lived in that neighborhood in the mid-1990s and I remember waiting, in 1995, for a car service that would deliver me to an executive education job. As I waited, I watched one angry, cursing man, waving a wood 2×4, chase another bleeding, cursing man out of a sidewalk stairwell and down the block. Emotional volatility and sudden bursts of violence weren't unusual in the neighborhood. Even now, after an economic transformation that has made the neighborhood alluring for those with money for luxurious apartments, high-end restaurants, and pricey retail, it is still an environment in which anxiety, obsession, and the self-centered pursuit of pleasure, wealth, and power seem more prevalent than the four guiding principles Pandit Dasa encourages us to remember: (1) forgiveness, (2) patience, (3) compassion, and (4) selflessness.

Pandit's early interest in mindfulness was catalyzed by a rough period as a young man in Bulgaria. He followed his father and mother to eastern Europe, with the goal of rebuilding the hard-earned family fortune after a catastrophic series of bad luck in Los Angeles. It was in Bulgaria that Pandit took the first steps that would contribute to his eventual years as a monk.

After returning with his parents to the United States, and working around New York City in unfulfilling jobs, Pandit decided he would travel to India at the recommendation of monks he met in NYC. He went on a spiritual journey that involved 100% commitment to earn the right to wear the saffron robes of a monk. What he brings us in this book are practical ways for us to benefit from the hard-earned wisdom of his journey as a monk.

Pandit experienced most of his youth, and his high school years, in the same area of Los Angeles where I had also been raised (many years earlier). Both of us spent our high school days in a very comfortable dream of the SoCal fantasy, our homes facing the distant Pacific Ocean to the west and the snowy peaks of the San Gabriel Mountains behind us to the northeast. Both of us grew up with fathers who fought to move from poverty to affluence. I only share this similarity in our backgrounds to emphasize the unique courage behind his choice. There are many career opportunities a young person might choose. Many of them offer great benefits to society, while rewarding the person, both personally and professionally, for their commitment to their chosen career. Pandit chose to spend 15 years of his adult life in the development of his mind and the service of helping other people improve their minds. He chose to ignore many available rewards and focus on the value of achieving a more centered, satisfied existence for himself and for others.

In November of 2019, Pandit shared his journey as a monk with the Columbia Business School Advanced Management Program (AMP), a four-week leadership development program for senior-level business leaders. I have been co-running the AMP for over 13 years. Pandit and I took very different paths in our lives, and probably because of the similar starting points and the different life choices, I could see that his knowledge was an important resource to the ongoing growth of the global business leaders we work to develop at Columbia Business School.

I am sure you will enjoy this book. Use the lessons, respond to the questions, apply his hard-earned insights. Pandit took a unique journey and he shares specific wisdom to help you confront adversity and help replace ego with empathy.

*Bruce Craven*<br>
*Faculty, CBS Executive Education*<br>
*Adjunct Associate Professor, Columbia Business School*<br>
*Author,* Win or Die: Leadership Secrets from Game of Thrones<br>
*(Thomas Dunne Books/St. Martin's Press, 2019)*<br>
www.cravenleadership.com

# Preface

It wasn't long after I finished my first book, *Urban Monk*, in 2013 that people began asking me about the plan and content of my second book. Getting through the whole process of writing and editing had turned out to be much more work than I had anticipated, and I wasn't even close to thinking about a second book. I felt that I had given what felt like everything to my first book and didn't have much more to say at the time. I definitely didn't want to force myself to write. I needed to be inspired from within to go down that road for a second time. It was also the time, in 2014, that I was beginning to ponder my exodus from the 15 years I had spent living as a monk in New York City. This was a big transitional phase in my life and a lot needed figuring out about how I was going to survive and function in the normal world.

It was during the 15th year of my monastic experience, after having given over 1,000 speeches and workshops centering around mindfulness and work–life balance on college campuses in New York and around the country, that I started getting invitations to speak at corporations and conferences. Not wanting to think about writing a second book, I dove into developing my corporate speaking and decided that I would wait for the right inspiration and content to develop before putting my thoughts down on paper. I began traveling around the country giving speeches at companies of all sizes, from startups to Fortune 500s, at company retreats and HR conferences.

In June of 2017, almost four years after my first book, I began to note down some ideas and casually began writing with the idea of eventually publishing another book. I got one-third to halfway through and then lost inspiration and continued to develop my speaking business. After most of my talks, people kept asking me when I would write a book on mindfulness as it applies to the workplace and I would just smile and respond, "hopefully soon." Pressure was building for me to continue writing, but somehow I just wasn't feeling the motivation to set aside time to sit myself down and seriously begin the writing process. However, I knew that as a speaker, it was absolutely crucial to come out with a second book that would expand on the topics that I was speaking on.

By some good fortune, in July of 2019, a mentor and friend, who had been a monk for almost 30 years, was visiting from India, so I thought to reach out and spend some time with him. I didn't plan to talk about my next book with him but decided to casually tell him that I had been working on a manuscript, that it had been sitting on my computer for almost two years, and that I could finish it in a few months if I really was determined to. He wasted no time and strongly encouraged me to finish it up and to not procrastinate any further. He actually told me to go home and write down my writing goals for the book and to note down a date by which I would finish writing. I followed his suggestions and right from the next day, started to write, and I met and exceeded my writing goals for each week. Within three months, I had completed the basic manuscript. He gave me the exact push that I needed to get this done. It's truly amazing how people go in and out of our life to inspire us and teach us. Some teach in a positive way and others in not such a positive way. However, they all come to teach. Fortunately, my mentor's encouragement was incredibly positive and gave me the inspiration to write. Our endeavor in all things is absolutely crucial; however, I do believe that things will happen as and when they're meant to and not a second earlier and not a second later.

In July 2020, during the early stages of the pandemic, I self-published my second book and called it *Closing the Apps: How to Be Mindful at Work and at Home*. "Closing the Apps" is a phrase that I was using during my corporate talks; it refers to the apps we have open in our mind and that if we learn to close these "apps," then we can reduce our stress levels and be more productive and happy in our work and personal life.

Between March 2020 and December 2022, I had delivered over 200 virtual talks for a variety of organizations and their employees located around the globe. Corporations were struggling to understand what the future of work would look like and how to help their employees with work–life balance and their mental health. The pandemic had caused a major disruption and was increasing stress and anxiety for employers and employees. Requests for virtual speeches to address these crucial topics started pouring in and I found myself quickly developing new topics and adjusting old ones for the current environment.

By the end of 2022, I realized I had developed much more content that needed to be added to *Closing the Apps*. Hence, during the months of December and January, I expanded the content of *Closing the Apps* and wrote a new edition.

In this new edition, I include topics on work–life balance, creating boundaries between work and personal life, and the very important subject of mental health and breaking the stigma surrounding it. Hence the new title, *Mindfulness For the Wandering Mind*.

CHAPTER **ONE**

# Covid, Work from Home, and Employee Well-Being

## Overview

Ever since Covid shut the world down in 2020, conversations surrounding mental health have come to the forefront like never before. For too long, people were afraid to talk about and address their mental and emotional health needs. There has been and continues to be a stigma around mental health that people feared would isolate them in the workplace and possibly make them look weak, inefficient, and unproductive. After all, the workplace isn't a space one wants to be vulnerable in and so workers would simply brush their mental health needs under the rug and just ignore them.

Social isolation forced everyone to talk about this topic because the matter could no longer be ignored. It was almost as if Covid revealed to society that many of us are actually struggling with our mental health even though we didn't think we were. We were forced to face this harsh reality. Covid either brought out our mental health struggles, helped to create them due to the uncertainty it put the world in, or possibly both.

Society worldwide got completely blindsided by the pandemic. This was the first time in human history that the entire human population shared a similar struggle. Perhaps for the first time, we could truly relate to each other. Generally, whenever we watch the news and learn about some part of the world experiencing a natural disaster, we quickly become indifferent to it and the suffering of the people there because our life isn't impacted. However, Covid was different, and it forced us to relate to each other like never before.

Not feeling comfortable going to a grocery story, walking the dog, simply going for a walk; being paranoid about touching any surface that might have been touched by another person and being mandated to wear a face mask were very unnatural additions to our lifestyle that were suddenly thrust upon us. In school, we had experienced fire and earthquake drills as a preparation for such events. Some parts of the world have drills preparing for bombs or war; however, most of the world has never undergone a pandemic drill and so we were thoroughly unprepared. One of my friends, who lived in the suburbs of New Jersey, barely came out of his house for an entire year. He and his family were afraid to even go into their backyard. When they received mail or Amazon deliveries, they would leave them in one part of their house for 24–48 hours before touching them. We went from thinking that Covid would pass in a few weeks to becoming completely paranoid about engaging in activities that once seemed completely normal.

For the first several months, I washed all our vegetables with hot water and even soap out of anxiety of getting Covid. Everything that came into the house was cleaned, wiped, or sprayed.

Pre-Covid, many dreamed of and romanticized the idea of working from home in their pajamas and how nice it would be to have the whole house to themselves, free to do as they please. Life gives us part of what we wish for, but it doesn't always give it to us in exactly the way we want. So, we got to work from home in the attire of our choice, for at least the lower part of our body, but we had our entire family at home with us, with everyone competing for work and study space.

Many liked the idea of being able to work from home, but for a majority, trying to get work done while having to tend to the needs of family, pets, and managing household chores, all at the same time, turned out to be a much more daunting task than anyone could have anticipated. We love our families but being around them 24/7 was much more than we were prepared for. In addition to a crowded home environment, people ended up working longer hours. Many felt pressured to put in extra hours because they didn't need to go into the office and felt a need to prove to their bosses that they weren't slacking off while they were at home. People's commute times became nonexistent, which translated into extra hours of work. Gone were the lunch hours, the casual conversations with colleagues, and the general camaraderie that exists in an office environment.

Then there were those without families, living in small apartments in big cities, who were bouncing off the walls and losing their minds because Covid was keeping them locked up in a tiny studio or one-bedroom apartment with little to no interaction with friends, families, or colleagues. Humanity was being severely tested and a global mental health crisis was emerging. This was something corporations could no longer ignore. Companies were realizing that if they didn't provide care for their employees' mental health, they would not only see a significant drop in productivity levels but they would also experience a large dropoff in retention numbers.

## Employee Mental Health

Covid gave individuals and corporations a huge wake-up call in terms of the importance of maintaining and managing the mental and emotional well-being of its workforce. These are core needs of humans, and companies began to realize that since an employee spends over half of their waking time at the workplace and since the workplace is responsible for a good chunk of the stress in a person's life, they needed to take partial responsibility to address and provide support for the mental health concerns of their employees. It seems only reasonable that if an organization is hiring someone and expecting them to dedicate a good portion of their mental, physical, and emotional energy into the workplace, there needs to be some reciprocation beyond just a paycheck. A paycheck is good, but it's not enough. Money can allow an individual to buy things to make their life comfortable and pay bills. It can also relieve a certain amount of stress we experience; however, it cannot replenish the mental and emotional exhaustion that can be experienced at the end of the workday or workweek.

A human being is more than a number and the productivity they bring into the workplace. They have a life outside of work that involves family, health, finances, social obligations, and so many other essential components. When companies focus only on the skillset and the productivity potential of the individual being hired or already in the organization and neglect the rest of what makes that person human, that creates a serious disconnect. Unfortunately, this is how most corporations have dealt with their employees in the past, but Covid helped sound an alarm that something needed to change with the attitude and approach an organization has toward its employees. The volcano of mental health was beginning to erupt and emergency measures were needed to bring this under control.

People were, more than ever before, ready to walk away from jobs that didn't provide the right care, environment, and work culture to help them thrive and remain happy in the workplace. Thus the "Great Resignation" started to take place in 2020 and 2021. According to Wikipedia, the main reasons for quitting were ". . . wage stagnation amid rising cost of living, limited opportunities for career advancement, hostile work environments, lack of benefits, inflexible remote work policies, and long-lasting job dissatisfaction.[1] My fiancée left her job at a major bank because they were unwilling to let her work from home and wanted everyone back in the office. I had moved to Florida from New Jersey while she was living in Columbus, Ohio. In order for her to make the move so we could be together, she found a job with another financial

[1]"Great Resignation," Wikepedia, https://en.wikipedia.org/wiki/Great_Resignation

institution that allowed for fully remote work. Many companies were able to make the adjustment to remote work while others refused to budge, ended up losing great talent to other organizations.

## Creating Boundaries While Working from Home

One of the biggest struggles people have faced while working from home is learning to create boundaries between when they start working and when they finish. Pre-Covid, one would physically walk out of the house to get to work and then walk out of the office and drive home. This ritual created a natural boundary between home and work life. The problem with the home office is that the boundary no longer exists and our workaholic tendencies can easily take over. Many find themselves starting work while eating breakfast, which is taking away from family time. This working pattern can easily spill over to dinnertime, which is crucial for deepening connections with loved ones. This is especially important while everyone is working and studying from home and tensions are on the rise.

In the many speeches I have been giving, during and post-Covid, I have been encouraging people to learn to create these boundaries. A lack of boundaries will lead to burnout and will negatively affect our personal relationships. Here are a few ways in which we can go about creating a divide between our work and personal life, while working from home:

1. Write down, on a Post-it Note or notepad, what time your workday will start and when it will end. Make sure the note is visible to you. Writing something down creates a greater level of commitment to follow through on it.

2. Make a note of when you'll take breaks during your workday. Additionally, write down how you plan to use your break time and what activity you will engage in. The last thing we want to do is have an unplanned break time and just spend that 10 minutes scrolling on your phone, because that's not letting our brain decompress. That's why it's best to tell yourself how you plan to keep your body active and get yourself to stop thinking about work-related activities during your break.
3. As much as possible, create a completely separate space in your home that is exclusively for work. This is a space dedicated to only work-related matters. When you walk away from this space during breaks or at the end of the workday, it'll feel like you just left work and are on your way home.
4. Take breaks throughout the day. If you're staring at screens all day long during work hours, try not to pull out your personal devices during these breaks so you can give your eyes and mind some relief. Some activities that can be done during these breaks:

    - Get up from your chair, move around, and take a brisk walk.
    - Do some exercise or yoga.
    - Meditate.
    - Take a short nap.

Robert Pozen, senior lecturer at MIT's Sloan School of Management, suggests that we take breaks every 75 to 90 minutes.

*We know that because we have studied professional musicians, who are most productive when they practice for this amount of time. It's also the amount of time of most college classes. Working for 75 to 90 minutes takes advantage of the brain's two modes: learning or focusing and consolidation. When people do a task and then take a break for 15 minutes they help their brain consolidate information and retain it better. That's what's happening physiology during breaks."*[2]

The research of Larissa Barber, PhD, who is an assistant professor of psychology at Northern Illinois University, and Amanda Conlin, who is studying social and industrial-organizational psychology at Northern Illinois University, is showing that for breaks to be effective, one needs to detach from work-related thoughts and activities and to experience "positive emotions."

Positive emotions reverse the negative effects of work tasks and increase blood flow to the areas in the brain that we use to focus.

Barber and Conlin also recommend avoiding certain breaktime activities, which can be counterproductive, such as drinking caffeine, snacking, or venting about a problem.[3]

---

[2]Stephanie Vozza, "This Is How Many Minutes of Breaks You Need Each Day," *Fast Company*, October 31, 2017. https://www.fastcompany.com/40487419/this-is-how-many-minutes-of-breaks-you-need-each-day

[3]Amanda Conlin and Larissa Barber, "Why and How You Should Take Breaks at Work," *Psychology Today*, April 3, 2017. https://www.psychologytoday.com/intl/blog/the-wide-wide-world-of-psychology/201704/why-and-how-you-should-take-breaks-at-work

The point is to disconnect and venting forces us to relive the incident, leading to further stress and fatigue. Some additional activities they suggest that can lead to a positive break experience are helping out a colleague, setting a new goal, or learning something new.

5. Avoid sending any and all work-related emails from your bed. Your bed isn't office furniture. By sending emails from our bed, we change the energy of the bedroom from something that is meant to unwind and relax us to something more active and productive. This can interfere with our sleep; we don't want our brains to get wired up right before going to sleep.
6. Keep all work-related devices in the dedicated workspace and not in the bedroom or other spaces meant for personal or family interaction.
7. Create a strict rule of not having devices at the dining table. Mealtime is a super-important opportunity to connect with family and have casual conversations. This rule also sets a very important example for kids because it's communicating to them that nothing is more important than family and family time – that getting together, talking to each other, and spending quality time with each other is the most valuable thing we can be doing.

## Summary

- Covid humbled us and made us realize that we don't have as much control as we think we do. It made us question our work environment and whether we need to be in the office five days a week. It sparked a conversation on workplace culture and what is healthy and what is toxic.

It brought to the forefront the much-needed discussion on our mental health, how much we have neglected it, and how important that aspect of our life is.

- Working from home while other members of the family are also around challenged us in ways we could not have imagined. It pushed us to explore and create boundaries between our work tasks and home responsibilities. In order for us to make it work, we realized that we would need to incorporate more wellness and self-care into each day.

## Reflection Questions and Exercises

Are you working from home and, if so, how has the experience been?

______________________________________________

______________________________________________

______________________________________________

What do you currently do to create boundaries between your work and personal life?

______________________________________________

______________________________________________

______________________________________________

Which of the techniques described in this chapter might be helpful for you in this regard?

______________________________________________

______________________________________________

______________________________________________

CHAPTER **TWO**

# The Pursuit of Work–Life Balance

## Overview

Learning to create the proper boundaries is the first step to having a healthy work–life balance. For those working from home, the lines between work and personal life have become increasingly blurred. The home can be filled with distractions, especially if both spouses are working from home. Developing a balance between our personal and professional responsibilities requires a certain amount of discipline and a desire to have a healthy life. One needs to be convinced that their family life, mental health, and emotional health need to become an absolute priority in order to experience happiness. It starts with evaluating our entire day, from the time we wake up till the time we go to sleep, and figuring out what adjustments need to be made.

It requires us asking ourselves questions such as "What nourishes me emotionally and spiritually?" and "What activities calm and relax me?" The next step is to do some introspection and write down all the answers we can. Then, we need to identify which of these activities can be easily, without much effort, implemented into our daily or weekly schedule. The key is to start off by adding small and easily achievable work–life balance activities into our routine so we can feel good about the progress we are making. The problem is that we aim too high too quickly. This leads to disappointment and frustration. Slow and steady is my motto when starting something new and especially when we want long-term sustainability. We also need to be careful to not add too many activities too quickly because of the initial excitement we might be feeling.

## The Best Way to Start the Day

The way we start the day sets the tone and mood for the rest of our day. How many of us are guilty of picking up our devices and scrolling through Instagram, TikTok, Facebook, and LinkedIn first thing in the morning, while still in bed? I know I'm guilty! It's become a habit that is going to be hard to part ways with. Going through the feed of many people's profiles filled with so many emotions isn't the best way to wake up our brain and mind. It's sort of like starting your car on a cold winter morning and pressing the pedal to the metal without giving it time to warm up. One problem with going through social media, especially first thing in the morning, is that we can end up getting depressed or even angry if we see friends vacationing in beautiful locations while we are about to head to work. With the presence of social media, it's hard to not compare ourselves with others. Comparing is something humans have always done. Deep down inside, we want to look and feel more accomplished than others. We have been engaging in this behavior since very early childhood.

When one sibling sees another sibling with a nicer toy, they will begin to throw a tantrum and, possibly, forcibly take away the toy. In school and in corporate life, we compare our clothes, cars, grades, looks, collection of gadgets, work titles, and salaries with everyone else's. With a few clicks, we can scroll through dozens of profiles within minutes and experience a huge plethora of feelings and emotions that can make us feel a bit exhausted even before getting out of bed. We don't want to start our morning already feeling stressed and anxious. Can we resist the temptation to grab our phone first thing in the morning and replace that activity with something more positive and energizing? Yes, we can! Here are a few suggestions for activities we can engage in right when we wake up.

- Take a few deep breaths to energize the body and mind and allow ourselves to gradually wake up.
- Allow ourselves to feel grateful for something positive happening in our life. Gratitude can immediately uplift us.
- Listen to some positive and uplifting music that can inspire us.
- Play a motivational and uplifting podcast that can provide us the inspiration, courage, and strength to get through the day.
- Do some stretching and yoga to warm up and get the body going.

- Avoid listening to or watching negative news first thing in the morning. According to the *Harvard Business Review*, "Just a few minutes spent consuming negative news in the morning can affect the entire emotional trajectory of your day."[1]
- Eat a healthy breakfast.

## Consuming a Healthy and Balanced Diet

Food is the fuel for our body. The amount of energy and mental clarity we have throughout the day will depend on the type of fuel we are putting into ourselves. If we're putting the wrong type of fuel into our vehicle, its life will get cut short and it won't perform as well in the long run. The vehicle won't help us get to our destination and the ride won't be very smooth. Unfortunately, we usually don't spend too much time on planning our meals and thinking about how the food we consume will impact our health and well-being. Once we start putting serious consideration into the food we eat, everything about the way we consume food will change.

If we have a heavy lunch, our energy level drops and it clogs our thinking and ability to make decisions. I have experienced this personally on multiple occasions, where I ate too much during lunch and went into a sort of food coma.

---

[1]Shawn Achor and Michelle Gielan, "Consuming Negative News Can Make You Less Effective at Work," *Harvard Business Review*, September 14, 2015. https://hbr.org/2015/09/consuming-negative-news-can-make-you-less-effective-at-work

There are four important components to consider when it comes to planning our meals and eating mindfully:

1. What we're going to eat
2. When we're going to eat
3. The quantity that will be consumed
4. How the meal will make us feel afterward

When meals aren't thought out, we will end up eating the tastiest items, which may not be the healthiest. If quantities aren't planned, we run the risk of overeating.

If we know we have an important meeting at 1 p.m., then it's important to consume a meal that will provide us with energy, focus, and clarity and won't slow down our thought process and produce a mental fog. It's also important to be mindful of how late we eat dinner. At the end of the day, after a long day's work, the body is fatigued and, as a result, the digestive system slows down. A heavy meal late in the evening is not a good idea. Whenever I have made the mistake of eating late, I find myself not getting a good night's sleep. The body spent the entire night trying to digest everything while I slept, which means my sleep wasn't as restful as it could have been and I woke up feeling full because not a whole lot got digested.

Moreover, all the meals we put into our body will affect our long-term health. Therefore, it is in our own self-interest to be mindful of our diet and what we put into our body.

### Increasing Our Intake of Plant-Based Foods

There is plenty of research supporting the idea that a plant-based diet can help reduce the risk of heart disease, diabetes, some types of cancers, and even mental illness:

> *Eating a plant-based diet improves the health of your gut so you are better able to absorb the nutrients from food that support your immune system and reduce inflammation. Fiber can lower cholesterol and stabilize blood sugar and it's great for good bowel management.*[2]

Even if we are increasing our consumption of plant-based foods, we still need to be mindful of the quantity of sugar and unhealthy fats we are consuming. Plant-based foods aren't limited to fruits and vegetables; they also include a variety of grains, nuts, seeds, and legumes. There is a whole world of food and eating that opens up as we begin to explore an adjustment to our diet. I have been on a plant-based diet since 1998, right before I became a monk. It's a diet I continue to maintain during my post-monk life, and I am glad to have made the switch.

For many, this adjustment is not an easy one, so it's best to take it slow, one meal at a time and one day at a time. Perhaps try out meatless Mondays and then gradually find ways to increase the amount of fruits, vegetables, grains, and legumes as part of your regular diet. Your body will thank you for it, and it's an amazing investment in your own physical and mental well-being.

## Getting a Good Night's Sleep

Work–life balance absolutely cannot exist if we are not getting enough rest each night. Of course, there will be nights when

---

[2]Heather Alexander, "5 Benefits of a Plant-Based Diet," University of Texas MD Anderson Cancer Center, November 2019. https://bit.ly/3PDae85

we don't get enough sleep for whatever reason, but that shouldn't become the norm. Sleep impacts not only our memory and mood but also our overall health and judgment. According to the National Institutes of Health, which is the nation's medical research agency:

> *Sleep deficiency is linked to many chronic health problems, including heart disease, kidney disease, high blood pressure, diabetes, stroke, obesity and depression.*[3]

The NIH research also shows that a lack of sleep can lead to more injuries in children, teens, and adults. Sleep deprivation hinders our ability to act with clarity and focus and has contributed to major accidents such as plane and car crashes and even nuclear reactor meltdowns. Sleep deprivation can lead us into hazardous situations in our personal life and in the workplace as well.

Pretty much all of our bodily functions will be impaired to some degree or other when our body is exhausted and sleep-deprived. Unfortunately, too often, in an aggressive and high-achieving corporate environment, people brag about the fact that they aren't sleeping enough and how they are able to function on only a few hours of sleep. People make such statements trying to demonstrate how tough or committed they are to the work. However, looking at the research, we can see that such statements are made out of ego and ignorance of how their body will react to the lack of rest. These statements are harmful for the culture of a workplace because

---

[3]"What Are Sleep Deprivation and Deficiency?," National Institutes of Health, March 24, 2022. https://bit.ly/3WnbzC2

they communicate to others that this is what is required to be successful. Moreover, it can isolate others, making them feel inadequate. Not getting enough sleep is nothing to brag about. We should actually be bragging when we get a good night's sleep and inspire others to do the same.

While there are no hard and fast rules as to how much sleep one should be getting each night – we all have different body types, bodily needs, and habits when it comes to work–life balance – the Centers for Disease Control and Prevention (CDC) suggests that teens should be getting between eight and 10 hours of sleep each night while adults 18 years and older should be getting seven hours of sleep.[4]

Like anything else, sleep requires a little planning and preparation. The more we prepare for it, the better quality and quantity of sleep we will achieve. It's all about making our health a priority and developing some positive habits to improve our sleep. While there are quite a few tips on getting a good night's sleep, I picked out my favorites from healthline.com.[5]

1. Get two hours of sunlight exposure during the day, which will keep us energized in the daytime, which will then help us get a good night's sleep.
2. Reduce bright lighting in your space during the evening, which lets your body know that the workday is coming to a close and it's time to start winding down. Bright lighting

[4]"How Much Sleep Do I Need?," Centers for Disease Control and Prevention, September 14, 2022. https://bit.ly/3v1TloC

[5]Rudy Mawer, "17 Proven Tips to Sleep Better at Night," *Healthline*, February 28, 2020. https://bit.ly/2HuJTW6

makes the brain think it's still daytime and that we need to remain productive.

3. Reduce exposure to "blue light," which is given off by smart devices. Blue light impacts your body's ability to produce the sleep hormone melatonin. There are settings on our devices that can automatically turn off the blue light in the evenings and turn back on in the morning. I have my blue light set to turn off at 9 p.m. and turn back on at 7 a.m.
4. Avoid consuming caffeine late at night. Caffeine can stay in our system for six to eight hours.
5. Take short daytime naps of 15 to 20 minutes, which can help recharge our energy levels – but naps that are longer can interfere with nighttime sleep.
6. To help the body maintain its circadian rhythm, it is best, if possible, to sleep and wake at regular times, including on weekends. It's natural to want to sleep in and catch up on rest during the weekend, but let's try our best to maintain a certain level of consistency as this will also be helpful when Monday morning comes around.
7. Avoid consuming alcohol before going to bed; alcohol can lower the production of melatonin, the hormone that helps us sleep.
8. Create as quiet and peaceful a space in your bedroom as you can and avoid doing any work-related activities while in bed.
9. It's best to eat at least three hours before going to bed, giving the body enough time to digest the food.
10. Exercise is great but not before going to bed. The idea is to relax the body and not get it all worked up.

Some additional activities we can implement to wind down and relax in the evening are taking a warm bath, drinking some warm and caffeine-free chamomile tea or other soothing beverage, reading a book, or listening to some calming music. When we turn off a table fan, the blades keep spinning. Similarly, our mind needs time to wind down and turn off and it can't do that the moment we turn off our work devices. Like any machine, the mind takes time to cool off. How long it takes depends on the individual and how intensely we were engaged. That's why it's important to plan backward. If you know that it takes you an hour or two to fully disconnect from work-related thoughts and you plan to go to sleep at 11 p.m., then you definitely want to be concluding work-related activities by 7 or 8 p.m. and hopefully earlier. This will give you time to wind down and spend some quality time with your family.

Most of these tips are fairly easy to implement. Getting a good night's sleep requires a little bit of planning and some discipline. Let's go ahead and select three of these practices that we can implement into our life this evening.

## The Importance of Positive Relationships

Probably the most important component of our life is having good, healthy relationships with our family, friends, and colleagues. Ultimately, we are working hard to earn a living so we can provide for our family and support our friends. The problem is that we often let our ambition to succeed take over and thus begin to neglect our family. We prioritize our work commitments over our personal ones. We tell ourselves and our family that "I'm doing this for the family." While there is truth to the statement that we are trying our very best to provide a comfortable life for our family, the greater truth is that, more than anything else, our family members need our time and personal presence. As the old adage goes, it's lonely at the top. We can have all the money, fame, and power in the world, but if we don't have people around us who care for us, it's all meaningless. The feeling of loneliness will eat away at our soul, and this is especially true when the holiday season comes around and as we begin to age. It's not impossible, but it gets harder to make new friends as we get older. People are very busy with their lives and commitments, and there is little time to dedicate for forming new relationships. During the holiday season, when everyone around us is celebrating with their loved ones and we haven't taken the time to cultivate such relationships, the loneliness will start to impact our mental, emotional, and physical health.

According to the CDC, adults 50 years of age and older are "socially isolated" or lonely in ways that puts their health at risk. Recent studies show that social isolation or loneliness can increase:[6]

- A person's chances of premature death
- Their chances of developing dementia by almost 50%
- Their risk of heart disease by 29%
- The chances of a stroke by 32%
- Depression, anxiety, and suicide, which are strongly associated with loneliness

[6] "Loneliness and Social Isolation Linked to Serious Health Conditions," Centers for Disease Control and Prevention, April 29, 2021. https://bit.ly/3Wjzra6

As we can see from this research, loneliness has a detrimental affect in every aspect of our physical and mental health. Relationships are by no means easy. They require tons of loyalty, commitment, and sacrifice. These traits are becoming rare in our modern culture, which naturally diminishes our chances of having healthy, long-term relationships where people are willing to stick with each other when things get difficult and challenging.

Having strong and caring relationships means being proactive in maintaining them, being willing to forgive the shortcomings of others and simultaneously work on our own imperfections. Relationships are like a tree. For it to grow strong and healthy, a tree requires a lot of watering, care, and the right amount of sunlight. It can literally take years before a tree will bear flowers and fruits. However, it can be cut down in minutes. Similarly, it can take months and years before we can fully trust someone and develop deep roots in that relationships, and too often, we can let one misunderstanding, miscommunication, or difference cut down that relationship. Every broken relationship, romantic or not, leaves a scar on our heart that may last a lifetime.

There are some relationships that we need to walk away from, especially if we have done everything possible to make them work but there is no tangible progress. This should not, however, be a whimsical decision but be the last resort. If there is a possibility of reconciling older relationships that have gone sour, we should explore those possibilities. It can be a very healing experience for our heart and soul.

## Building Strong and Sustainable Relationships

A major component of the word "life" in the phrase "work–life balance" is relationships. Ultimately, what is life without loving relationships? One could even argue that life and relationships are synonymous. As the research shows, our brain, mind, and heart are all affected when relationships are lacking. Humans aren't meant to live alone and be socially isolated. There are a few exceptions, such as monks who live in isolation in forests, but that is not an example we are meant to follow. Most monks live in monasteries with other monks. We all need like-minded individuals to relate to and experience life with. The most satisfying part of my 15 years as a monk was living with other monks; experiencing that camaraderie and serving society together was incredibly fulfilling. When most of the monks left the monastery for different reasons, I also left because trying to serve alone wasn't inspiring.

A good question to ask ourselves is how many true relationships do I have in my life. How many would be there for me if I were sick or in the hospital? Would people take time out of their busy schedules to visit me, sit by my side, and comfort me? If I needed someone to talk to, how many are there that would answer my call instead of sending it to voicemail? How many would make me their priority when the time comes?

Asking these questions can be uncomfortable. Even if we have only two or three people in our life who would be there for us during the rainy season, then we should really consider ourselves fortunate. It also means that we have done something right in maintaining those relationships. Another question to ask is how many people would call on me when they're going through a rough patch? Have I made myself available to others in the past so they feel comfortable reaching out, or have I kept myself aloof and indifferent? Have I been a reliable friend and relative?

Even if we haven't, it's never too late to change. Changing ourselves is probably the biggest task that lies ahead of us because it's so hard to make changes in our character and behavior. There are habits and tendencies that we have been carrying around for so much of our life, and it's extremely difficult to shed them. We have tried and sometimes achieved success and, at other times, fallen back into the same patterns. In my opinion, every effort to change is powerful and shows that we are recognizing that change is needed. Too many people go throughout their life not even conscious of the adjustments they need to make. Looking at one's self isn't easy. Seeing another's faults and deficiencies is actually quite easy, but looking in the mirror is hard. However, if we are determined to alter our behavior, we need to be honest and humble, and that is when powerful revelations will take place.

We might need someone to provide us feedback on how we can improve on a personal or professional front. This requires being vulnerable and having a certain amount of trust. If we have someone we can trust and someone who, in a mature and sensitive manner, can provide this feedback to us, then we can consider ourselves fortunate and begin working on ourselves in a deep and meaningful way. Working on ourselves loudly communicates to others that we value our relationship and are willing to go the extra mile to make things work.

## The Five Love Languages

Relationships are reciprocal in nature. Generally, we get back what we put into them. It's unreasonable to invest very little time and energy in our relationships and then expect a lot back. However, too often, we expect a much bigger return than our investment because we convince ourselves that we have done a lot for the other person when that may not be the case or the other party may not see it the same way. What is a lot and what isn't can vary tremendously depending on each person's perspective. There are different love languages, according to Gary Chapman, PhD, and author of *The Five Love Languages*. He explains that there are five ways in which people receive and express love:

1. Words of affirmation
2. Quality time
3. Gifts
4. Acts of service
5. Physical touch[7]

The key is understanding what the love language is of the person you are giving love to. It's not about how we want to give love but more about how the other wants to receive it. It's natural to think that the other will receive love the same way you like to receive love. If we are being attentive and thoughtful, we will make the effort to understand the love language of the other to make the connection more meaningful. It's equally important that we are able to communicate our love language to those close to us. Otherwise, over time, each side is going to

[7]Gary Chapman, *The Five Love Languages: The Secret to Love That Lasts*, Manjul Publishing House, 2001.

feel unloved and uncared for when the other party is feeling like they are doing everything they can.

According to *The 5 Languages of Appreciation in the Workplace* by Gary Chapman and Paul White (Northfield Publishing, 2011), the concept of love languages also applies in the workplace especially, when it comes to the way appreciation is expressed.[8] Showing appreciation is always a great practice. However, the way we express that appreciation is crucial. If someone is introverted and doesn't like public praise and we think they will love it, we will most likely end up making them feel very uncomfortable and even embarrassed. Therefore, it is vital for those in management to invest in and get to know their people and their personalities and engage accordingly if they hope to create a cohesive and trusting team.

Relationships are complicated and require constant work and attention. They require empathy and for us to try and step into the other's shoes to understand their perspectives and feelings. This is hard to do because everyone is so absorbed in their own life that it's challenging to make time to try to understand other people's perspectives. Stepping into someone else's shoes is much more challenging than we can imagine. How can we possibly step into the shoes of another when we don't know what kind of life experiences they have had, which has transformed them into who they are today? We are quick to judge and form opinions without knowing about the obstacles and upbringing the other has undergone. Judging is easy. Getting to know someone requires lots of time and effort, which are two things we are not always willing to give.

---

[8]Gary Chapman and Paul White, *The 5 Languages of Appreciation in the Workplace*, Northfield Publishing, 2011.

This is precisely why leadership can be a difficult position to be in. There are so many tasks and deadlines that need to be taken care of and there's never enough time. It's easy to tell others what to do and provide feedback for things that haven't been done correctly, but it's not easy to develop deep and trusting relationships, without which it's hard to show empathy and care. If those in leadership can make it a priority to take the time to comprehend the love language of their colleagues, they will build a strong and loyal team around themselves.

## Listening to Understand and Not to Respond

Whether it's a personal relationship, a professional one, or even a political one, the foundation of strong communication is going to be crucial. The breakdown of communication between two individuals can lead to mistrust, which can ultimately end in a break of that relationship. When communication falls apart on a political level, the consequences can be disastrous and can impact millions. Generally when we think of communication, we think of expressing our ideas, needs, and concerns in a clear and understandable manner. This is certainly true. An equal, if not a more important, component of any dialogue is listening to understand and not to respond.

Listening to understand requires a lot of practice. We start formulating responses to what others are saying before they have had a chance to complete their thought process. The problem with this is that when our brain starts creating responses, we are no longer able to hear what others are saying. The brain can only do one thing at a time; we don't multitask very well. If we could, then texting and driving wouldn't be a problem. In our society, the multitasking of texting and driving is getting us into accidents and killing us. To fully listen to and understand the other person means stopping our mind from coming up with a response while the other is still expressing their thoughts and concerns. Otherwise, we haven't fully heard what they have to say. Not only that, when we formulate a response, we are also not fully able to be attentive to other people's facial expression, tone of voice, and body language. These three items are crucial to pay attention to during any communication. It's through these items that we understand how strongly someone feels about an issue.

When we don't pay attention to all these items, we won't be able to fully hear and comprehend their message. This means that our response to the other person will not address their concerns, leaving them feeling unheard, uncared for, and disrespected. I am guilty of coming up with responses while others are speaking. In the beginning, I wasn't even aware that I was doing this. Eventually, I became aware of this tendency. Then I started to actively stop my mind from coming up with responses while others were still talking. It's not easy because the mind is like a runaway train that is hard to stop. However, it is our mind and we can control it to some degree.

Our fear is that we don't want to forget the response that is forming in our mind. However, from my experience, every time I have chosen to fully hear someone out, my response has always been better and the other party felt heard, which resulted in greater trust in the relationship.

## Summary

- Self-care isn't selfish and is an essential component of work–life balance. There is no reason for us to feel guilty for taking care of our physical, mental, and emotional needs. Caring for others starts with caring for ourselves. There is no magic formula for creating work–life balance. It requires that we be attentive to many aspects of our life.
- We need to be attentive to the quality and quantity of our sleep and do what we can to make sure we are getting enough rest. Otherwise, we will be doing a disservice not only to ourselves but to our family and colleagues.
- Consuming the right diet can have a major impact on our energy and focus levels, since food is the fuel for our body. It's important to be mindful of what we eat, how much we eat, how often we eat, and what time we eat.

- At least as important, if not more so, is the pursuit and maintenance of positive relationships in our life. Relationships, both professional and personal, require a lot of time, attention, patience, and acceptance. Having good relationships requires that we listen more than we speak and listen to understand and not just to respond.

## Reflection Questions and Exercises

### *Starting the Day*

What's the first thing you do when you wake up?

________________________________________

________________________________________

Write down three things you can do differently when you wake up that will give your day a positive start.

________________________________________

________________________________________

________________________________________

### *Healthy Diet*

What are some products you would like to cut out of your diet?

________________________________________

________________________________________

What healthy items can you add to your diet?

________________________________________

________________________________________

What time of day is your last meal? Is it at least three hours before you go to bed?

Write down which of your meals, over the next seven days can be plant-based. Try to repeat that for each week thereafter and gradually increase the number of plant-based meals.

| | Breakfast | Lunch | Dinner |
|---|---|---|---|
| **Monday** | | | |
| **Tuesday** | | | |
| **Wednesday** | | | |
| **Thursday** | | | |
| **Friday** | | | |
| **Saturday** | | | |
| **Sunday** | | | |

***Sleep***

How many hours of sleep do you currently get?

How many hours would you like to get?

Which of the techniques mentioned in this chapter can you implement this evening to improve your sleep?

___

___

___

***Developing Positive Relationships***

How many strong and trusting relationships do you have in your life and who are they with?

___

___

What can you do to deepen the relationships you currently have?

___

___

___

___

Are there people you would like to reconnect with, and who are they?

___

___

Do you feel you have taken the time to understand the love language of your family, friends, and colleagues?

________________________________________

________________________________________

What can you do to be the person others reach out to when they're in need?

________________________________________

________________________________________

**Further Reading**

Cathy Cassata, "Michael Phelps: 'My Depression and Anxiety Is Never Going to Just Disappear,'" Healthline. May 17, 2022. https://www.healthline.com/health-news/michael-phelps-my-depression-and-anxiety-is-never-going-to-just-disappear#Erasing-stigma

"Faces of Depression: Philip Burguieres," *Depression: Out of the Shadows + Take One Step: Caring for Depression, with Jane Pauley*, PBS, 2008. https://www.pbs.org/wgbh/takeonestep/depression/faces-philip.html

Jade Scipioni, "NBA Star Kevin Love on Finding Success While Struggling with Mental Health: 'You Can't Achieve Yourself Out of Depression,'" *CNBC Make It*. https://www.cnbc.com/2021/11/18/nba-star-kevin-love-on-mental-health-struggles-success-getting-covid.html

CHAPTER **THREE**

# Breaking the Mental Health Stigma

## Overview

More than ever before, highly successful and accomplished individuals are starting to speak up about their mental health struggles. This is helping others to start talking about their own challenges with their mental and emotional well-being. For too long, everyone has been embarrassed to talk about feeling depressed and anxious. However, we are slowly beginning to realize that just as the body can experience ups and downs in health, so can the mind. Not being able to openly discuss and address mental health challenges and keeping our feelings bottled up only makes things worse. Everything in life has its ups and downs and highs and lows and that is nothing to be ashamed of. Taking care of our physical body but not being attentive to the needs of our mind is equivalent to taking our car to the car wash but never looking under the hood to address the needs of the engine.

People who struggle with mental illness are often marginalized and made to look weak and incapable. However, in recent years, some of the most athletic and recognized people on the planet have begun opening up about their personal struggles with depression.

## Michael Phelps

With a total of 28 medals, of which 23 are gold, Michael Phelps is considered to be the most decorated Olympian of all time. In June 2016, he became the first-ever American swimmer to qualify for five Olympic teams. In the year 2000, he also became the youngest male Olympian since 1932. In 2008, he set an Olympic record by winning eight gold medals.[1]

In a *Healthline* article, he says:

> *My depression and my anxiety is never going to just disappear. I'm never going to be able to snap my fingers and say "Go away. Leave me alone." It makes me. It is a part of me. It's always going to be a part of me. . . .*[2]

He explains that throughout his swimming career, he had 10 people on hand helping him get stronger and paying close attention to his physical health. He didn't receive the same level of care and attention for his mental health. After living with depression, anxiety, and even suicidal thoughts for years and after receiving his second driving while under the influence of alcohol (DUI) offense in 2014, he decided he needed to start paying as much attention to his mental health as he was his physical health. He admitted himself to a treatment facility where he spent the next 45 days getting treatment for his mental health. This kind of step takes a high level of honesty, vulnerability, and courage, and a desire to not remain a victim and make excuses.

He wasn't some unknown person who only needed to worry about what the neighbors and family would think; he was known by the world. After he left the facility, he said that

---

[1]Michael Phelps, https://www.teamusa.org/usa-swimming/athletes/michael-phelps

[2]Cathy Cassata, "Michael Phelps: 'My Depression and Anxiety Is Never Going to Just Disappear,'" *Healthline*, May 17, 2022. https://www.healthline.com/health-news/michael-phelps-my-depression-and-anxiety-is-never-going-to-just-disappear#Erasing-stigma

"I started feeling like a person . . . I guess I could love myself and like who I saw."

## Naomi Osaka

Born to a Haitian father and a Japanese mother, and raised in Japan until the age of three, Naomi Osaka became the first Asian player to achieve top world rankings in the Women's Tennis Association. She became a professional tennis player at the very young age of 15. She was also the first player from Japan to win a Grand Slam title and has won a total of four Grand Slam titles, two U.S. Open titles, and two Australian Open titles. One of her most noted victories came in 2018 when she defeated one of her childhood idols, Serena Williams, in straight sets. She became ranked number one in the world in 2019 and held that ranking for 21 weeks.[3] Along with many other accolades, she won the Associated Press "Female Athlete of the Year" award in 2020.

Naomi admitted to having long struggled with anxiety and depression and when she chose to skip the press interview at Roland-Garros, she received heavy criticism from the press. Her reason for wanting to withdraw from the press conference was to provide mental health self-care. She explained that the traditional press conference style is outdated and needed to be revamped to be a little more friendly and enjoyable on both sides. She feels that while athletes have a duty to the media, they should be allowed to take a mental break from them. When the press and tournament didn't believe that she needed

---

[3]"Naomi Osaka," Britannica, March 3, 2023. https://www.britannica.com/biography/Naomi-Osaka

a mental health break from media interviews, she felt tremendous pressure to disclose her symptoms. She has missed only one press conference. She feels that, just as in any workplace, where an employee receives a certain number of sick days without having to explain the specific symptoms they are experiencing, athletes should be given the same courtesy. She feels that athletes should be allowed a certain number of "sick days" from the press where they are not required to reveal their reasons.

She acknowledges that she is an introvert and finds it difficult to be in the spotlight. Speaking up for what she believes in is not something that comes easily to her. Many might find this hard to believe because she performs on a world stage, which is something that adds additional stress and anxiety to her mental health. Living with so many expectations and always being under a microscope can't be easy for anyone, especially if they don't like the spotlight. Naomi received tremendous support from many prominent personalities for speaking up and speaking out, some of whom are Michelle Obama, Michael Phelps, Steph Curry, Novak Djokovic, and Meghan Markle. She said that Michael Phelps told her that by speaking up, she may have saved a life.[4]

## Ben Simmons

Born in Melbourne, Australia, Ben Simmons joined the National Basketball Association (NBA) in 2016, after spending one year

---

[4]Naomi Osaka, "It's O.K. Not to be O.K.," *TIME*, July 8, 2021. https://time.com/6077128/naomi-osaka-essay-tokyo-olympics/

playing for Louisiana State University, where he was named rookie of the year. He was drafted first overall by the Philadelphia 76ers to play the position of point guard. When Simmons wasn't able to play, citing mental health reasons, the fans in Philadelphia and the media didn't react to the announcement with kindness. Some even criticized him for using mental health as an excuse for sitting out of training camp and part of the regular season due to a personal feud he was having with the Philadelphia 76ers. Simmons even expressed that "A bunch of things that were going on over the years, I wasn't myself. It wasn't about the basketball, it wasn't about the money."

The Sixers had offered help but Simmons turned down that help, stating that "Philadelphia does not have a mental health doctor on its staff with whom Simmons is comfortable." Instead he chose outside help, finding his own mental health practitioner, which allowed him greater privacy and where he wouldn't feel pressured to return to work immediately. Ben Simmons was even criticized, after he was traded to the Brooklyn Nets in 2022, for looking like he was smiling and enjoying himself while sitting on the sidelines at the Barclays Center.[5]

The criticism can be completely ridiculous and harsh. It's a good indication of how ignorant the public can be and how little we understand about the implications of mental health on an individual. People with mental health struggles are allowed to smile, feel good, and have fun. Just because they are having

---

[5] Julie Kliegman, "Ben Simmons's Mental Health Is Not a Joke," *SI*, February 15, 2022. https://bit.ly/3WDQUKz

fun doesn't mean things aren't really tough. We are quick to form judgments of others based on a quick moment in their life. Seeing someone smiling and waving the peace sign on Instagram doesn't mean that everything in their life is good and perfect. A little scratch can reveal a lot more than what we see on the surface. Ideally, when we see someone who is struggling with their mental health, smile, we should feel happy for them.

Sports fans can be especially brutal because they are paying money to watch their favorite athletes play and they often forget that athletes are also regular people with families and personal issues that they need to deal with, just like us. When fans don't get what they want, they can turn on an athlete in an instant. This turn of events from being loved to being hated overnight can take a very serious toll on the mental health of athletes. It's easy to say that we shouldn't care what others think about us or that "words will never hurt us," but the reality is that we do care what others think and words can hurt and even scar us for a very long time. This is especially true when the number of people who are thinking and forming opinions about us and talking about us publicly on social media number in the millions. One can't be expected to simply ignore that and not be affected by that. Hardly anyone on the planet has that strong or callous of a mind. Even the greatest yogis and meditators would have a difficult time with that. Sports is a very difficult profession to be in. Everything has an up and downside, as does fame. One moment you're flying high and the next moment, you can come crashing down in a memorable fashion for the whole world to witness. Additionally, because athletes earn such a ludicrous amount of money, it makes it hard for the public to emphasize with and feel sorry for them.

## Simone Biles

Simone Biles is one of most accomplished American gymnasts of all time, with 32 medals (19 gold). She has won four Olympic gold medals and is the "first female gymnast to earn three consecutive World All-Around titles. She is a three-time recipient of the Laureus World Sports Award for Sportswoman of the Year and has received widespread recognition, including *TIME* 100 Most Influential, *Forbes* 30 Under 30, *Ebony* Power 100, *People* Women Changing the World, *USA Today* 100 Women of the Century, and two-time Associated Press Female Athlete of the Year, among others."[6]

Simone Biles is no stranger to the spotlight and the pressures felt by elite athletes to perform and entertain, especially when they are representing their nation during the Olympic games. The expectations placed on them are tremendous and would probably be too much for most to handle. She has been in the competitive world of gymnastics from the age of 14. She shocked the world during the 2020 Tokyo Olympic games, when she withdrew from the Olympic games due to the tremendous amount of stress she experienced. After this happened, people began to approach her on the street to congratulate her, not for the multiple gold medals or for being the most decorated Olympic gymnast of

[6]Simone Biles, https://simonebiles.com/

all time, but for having the strength and courage to prioritize her mental health over her highly competitive work.[7]

This is truly a leader leading by example. She is setting the right example for not only other high-performing athletes but for everyone. We can't live our lives simply to live up to everyone else's expectations of us. We need to keep our finger on the pulse of our mental health and do what is best for us in the long run. The truth is that most people will have expectations of us but don't really care about us and what happens to us. In the case of professional athletes, people are just looking for entertainment and when one athlete can't give it to them, they will jump to someone else to find that entertainment. We are responsible for our well-being and that needs to be prioritized over everything else.

Whether one is in the spotlight or living a normal life with a 9-to-5 job, our mental health needs to remain a priority, and this is the message we can take from the example of Simone Biles. Withdrawing from the Olympics must have been an incredibly difficult decision that she probably lost sleep over and pondered very deeply. However, she knew what would be best for her career and personal life in the long run. Often, we need the right guidance in our life, from those who have our main interest in mind, to help us make the tough decisions. It is critical that those guiding us aren't motivated by their own self-interest when offering advice and suggestions.

Simone relies on and encourages others to utilize their support system of close family and friends. She further adds

---

[7]Sara Tardiff, "Simone Biles Called Dropping Out of the Tokyo Olympics Her 'Biggest Win,'" *Teen Vogue*, April 14, 2022. https://bit.ly/3jLJ6Yz

that even though we may be afraid or hesitant to ask for help, we can't go it alone. She also relies on therapy and uses the mental health app Cerebral.

## Kevin Love

Kevin Love's basketball career began at the Lake Oswego High School in Oregon, where he became the all-time leading scorer in the history of the school. During that time, he also earned the title of male high school athlete of the year. He continued his basketball career when he played for the UCLA Bruins, where he only spent one year before turning pro and entering the NBA draft. He was selected fifth overall by the Memphis Grizzlies in 2008. He has been selected as an NBA All-Star five times and has won an NBA championship in 2016 with the Cleveland Cavaliers while playing alongside LeBron James.[8]

In an essay for *The Players' Tribune*, Kevin Love details his decades-long struggle with mental health and the panic attack he had during the middle of an NBA game that was the catalyst that made him realize that he couldn't let the past remain buried and that he needed to get therapy and start to uncover the pains from the past. He provides great details of his panic attack. He explains that he was already experiencing stress from some family-related issues and on top of that, his team's season had gotten off to a slow start, with more losses than wins. He could tell that he wasn't himself right from the start of the game and he wasn't playing the way he normally would. During the third-quarter timeout, while sitting on the

[8]"Kevin Love," Lines, https://www.lines.com/nba/players/kevin-love-572

bench, he could feel his heart beat faster than usual and he was struggling to catch his breath. He further goes on to describe that everything around him was spinning and that his mouth felt like chalk. At that time, he knew he couldn't possibly get back on the court and he ran to the locker room. He noticed that his heart wouldn't stop racing and he felt like he was going to die. Eventually, he ended up on the floor of the training room just trying to get enough air. The Cavs took him to the Cleveland Clinic where they ran several tests and everything seemed fine. He remembers leaving the hospital thinking, *"Wait . . . then what the hell just happened?"*[9]

A couple of days later, he was back on the court and played a great game, scoring 32 points. He remembers feeling relieved that no one knew about his panic attack. He didn't want to be perceived by the team and the public as weak or as an unreliable teammate. As an athlete of that caliber, you're supposed to be able to tough it out and just move on. However, this incident was a big aha moment in his life and he decided it was time to get help. The Cavs helped him find a therapist. He went to the appointment with skepticism and one foot out the door. However, he was pleasantly surprised by the experience and by all the "nonbasketball" issues that began to surface. Love explains that an NBA athlete is surrounded by nutritionists, trainers, and coaches, but none of them could help him when he was lying on the floor of the locker room struggling to breathe.

---

[9]Kevin Love, "Everyone Is Going Through Something," *The Players' Tribune*, March 6, 2018. https://bit.ly/3vFbyxK

Kevin Love has taken a well-rounded approach toward his mental health which, in addition to therapy, includes good sleep, a healthy diet, working out, and meditation. He says that ever since he openly began talking about mental health, more people have approached him about this topic than about basketball.

When highly successful individuals, such as the ones mentioned earlier, openly talk about the challenges with their own mental health and how they're dealing with it, it begins to normalize the conversation around mental health. It helps break the stigma that mental illness is synonymous with weakness and incompetence. Mental illness doesn't discriminate. Anxiety and depression can and do impact people of all ages, backgrounds, and vocations. Our profession doesn't have much to do with our mental health. Of course, a very stressful and toxic environment, in any field of work, can definitely contribute to the worsening of our mental health.

According to the Centers for Disease Control (CDC) and the National Alliance on Mental Illness (NAMI)[10]:

- 1 in 5 U.S. adults experience mental illness each year
- 1 in 20 U.S adults experience serious mental illness each year
- 1 in 6 youth aged 6–17 experience a mental health disorder each year

According to the World Health Organization, "Depression is a common illness worldwide, with an estimated 3.8% of the

[10]"Mental Health By the Numbers," National Alliance on Mental Illness, June 2022. https://www.nami.org/mhstats

population affected, including 5.0% among adults and 5.7% among adults older than 60 years. Approximately 280 million people in the world have depression."[11]

Seeing these statistics hopefully helps us understand that we are not alone in this struggle.

According to the Mayo Clinic, there are multiple causes of mental illness. One such cause can start even while we're in the womb, if we were exposed to drugs, alcohol, toxins, and environmental stressors, which can be linked to mental illness. It can be inherited from family members who also have mental illnesses. Life situations such as financial struggles, divorce, death of a loved one, prolonged medical conditions, childhood abuse or neglect, and unhealthy social environments can lead to the development of mental illness.

## How to Recognize Symptoms of Depression

Feeling lonely, sad, anxious, and even depressed once in a while is fairly normal for most human beings. Life won't go the way we want it to a lot of times and when that happens, it is natural for us to feel down and disheartened. Occasionally feeling this way is normal in the course of life. Just like there are days and night and winters and summer seasons, there will be ups, downs, highs, and lows in our moods and emotions. This isn't something to be worried about. No one can be expected to be cheerful and happy all the time. That wouldn't be normal.

---

[11]"Depression," World Health Organization, September 13, 2021. https://www.who.int/news-room/fact-sheets/detail/depression

Some signs to look out for, in ourselves or others, that may indicate signs of depression and mental illness are:

- Feeling hopeless and pessimistic
- Prolonged sadness and anxiety
- Not wanting to get out of bed
- Loss of interest in things we previously enjoyed
- Loss of appetite or overeating
- Suicidal thoughts
- Fatigue
- Having trouble concentrating

One of the first things to do if we or a loved one is experiencing such symptoms is to talk to a medical professional who could prescribe a variety of treatments, including medication. Some activities we can engage in to improve our own mental health are:

- Getting enough sleep
- Eating a healthy diet
- Having positive relationships
- Meditation
- Yoga and exercise

When we see a loved one experiencing mental illness, there are certain statements we avoid saying. Too often, we just don't know how to respond and how to support them. Any message that minimizes or is dismissive of their mental health should be avoided, such as "just be positive," "it could've been worse," "so many others are going through much more," "it's all in your head," or "just snap out of it."

Many won't ask for help out of feelings of embarrassment or perhaps they just don't know how to ask for help. One of the most important things we can do is to not make them feel like they are being judged. That will only close them off from us and possibly from getting help altogether. An important thing to keep in mind is that we can't force anyone to get help. That's a decision they need to make on their own. However, we can definitely make ourselves accessible and let them know that we are available to have a conversation with them. Some practical steps we can take in providing help:

- Help them find a therapist or other medical professional.
- Offer to accompany them to the appointment.
- Provide assistance with day-to-day tasks.
- Be a good listener.
- Let them know you're there for them.

If someone is considering hurting themselves, call the suicide hotline or take them to the hospital.

It's very difficult to understand what someone with depression goes through on a daily basis and how hard it can be for them to get out of bed and get through the day. The best thing we can do is educate ourselves about depression and do our best to be kind and understanding with ourselves and with those going through it.

## Summary

- There has been a tremendous stigma around mental health. People avoid talking about their mental health because they don't want to get labeled, and we know that labels can be hard to remove. It's much easier for us to talk about going to a dentist or some other medical professional, but most are reluctant to openly talk about seeing a therapist or taking medications for mental health.

- Conversations regarding mental health have progressed in a positive direction thanks to highly successful athletes coming forward to address their own struggles with depression and anxiety. Athletes such as Michael Phelps, Naomi Osaka, Ben Simmons, Simone Biles, Kevin Love, and many others are showing the world that one can be highly competitive, accomplished, and literally the best on the planet and still have challenges with mental health. They are helping take the shame out of it, which is making it possible for others to open up about it as well.

## Reflection Questions and Exercises

How do you feel about your own mental health?

________________________________________

________________________________________

Do you have people in your life that you could open up to and have a conversation with about your mental and emotional well-being?

________________________________________

________________________________________

Are there people in your personal and/or professional life that might need help?

____________________________________________

____________________________________________

How can you start a conversation letting them know you're there for them?

____________________________________________

____________________________________________

____________________________________________

____________________________________________

CHAPTER **FOUR**

# Closing the Apps of the Mind

## Overview

The mind is the control center for human functioning. It controls our mood, emotions, speech, responses, and overall behavior. Like a smart device, it has a lot of apps running in the background that are draining our energy and if we don't learn to close out the negative apps, we will be left depleted, both physically and emotionally. This chapter explores the nature of the mind and how to close out the unneeded apps.

When we talk about mindfulness, it is useful to address these basic questions: What is the mind, what is the nature of the mind, and how do we begin to understand what the mind is?

## The Hard Drive

I like to compare the mind to a hard drive, which can store millions and millions of files. Similarly, the human brain can process and retain more data than we could ever imagine, and science still cannot fully explain how this organ operates. Each time we see, smell, taste, or touch something, the experience is recorded in our mind, regardless of our level of awareness. Even the many sights and sounds that we grow accustomed to and ignore are still mentally photographed and stored. There isn't anything the mind doesn't register.

For example, when I lived on the Lower East Side of Manhattan, the noise of cars, people talking, sirens, and even construction were so constant that I no longer noticed them. However, these sounds still entered into the deep recesses of my mind. Just as a camera captures everything in its purview even though we are focusing on one specific object, our mind absorbs all it comes in contact with.

## Apps in the Mind

The mind also functions like applications, or apps, on a smartphone or tablet. On our smart device, we have installed dozens of apps. Too often we open an app and forget to close it out, resulting in multiple apps running simultaneously in the background that we really don't need. We might have used Google Maps several days back, but after reaching our destination, we never bothered to shut it off.

So, what happens to our devices when all of these unused programs are operating? With each application using precious space and energy, processing speeds slow down and batteries begin to drain. At this point, a reset is needed. We need to close out the excess apps, perform a complete reboot, and when the device comes back on, we can feel the difference in how smoothly it operates.

**Closing out the apps to improve focus**

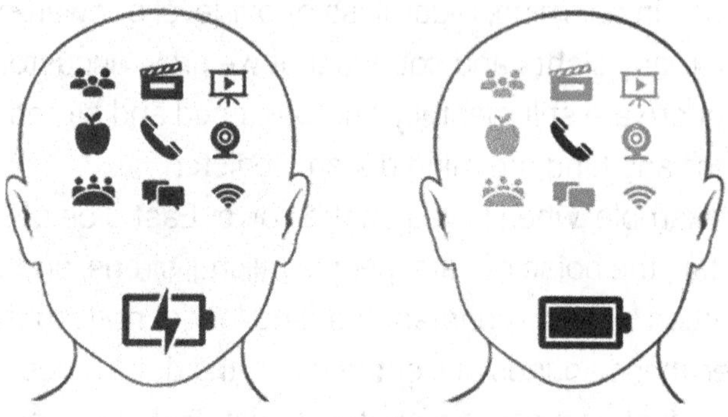

Like a smartphone, our mind winds up having a lot of apps open, and similarly, some of these factory-installed apps can't be deleted. There is the Money app, which regularly whispers to us that we do not have enough. Then there is the Food app, which cleverly has us thinking about our next meal, where we can get it, and how tasty we hope it will be. However, like our phone, if we can close some of these apps that we instinctively leave open, then our mind can function with greater clarity and focus.

## The Meandering Mind

Taking a more organic approach, there is the scattered nature of the mind. Like a set of windshield wipers, our thoughts go back and forth from the past to the future while hardly ever being in the present. Many times, the mind has an unfortunate tendency to get stuck on the negative moments we have experienced.

How many of us are bothered by events that happened a year ago? Five years ago? When I ask my audience these questions, almost everyone raises their hand in affirmation. We don't want to dwell on these negative things, and if we could, we would fully let them go. Yet, these unpleasant thoughts suddenly pop into our minds when we are having a good time with friends or family. We could be sitting on a beach in Hawaii, and something random can trigger the remembrance of an event from the past. Before we know it, we no longer see the beach or hear the sounds of the waves crashing against the sand. Instead, we are deeply immersed in reliving a painful situation, a memory that can last for a few minutes or several days, haunting us and ruining our vacation.

Without any warning, our mind is constantly meandering on random paths that are often irrelevant to our life. It's as if an entirely different person lives in our head, like a crazy roommate that we let move in without checking references and who never shuts up. When this happens, we begin to understand how little control we have over our mind, which is currently functioning on autopilot. The old files it decides to open up and dive into are completely out of our hands.

## Mind Over Matter

Even more fundamental, the mind has a tremendous amount of influence over our physical health. One simple way to understand the power of the body–mind connection is when we experience a nightmare. We do not choose to have a bad dream – for some unknown reason, our brain decides to play a horror movie during the deepest part of our sleep, and we have no choice but to suffer through it. Upon awakening, we find our heart rate is increased, and we are breathing faster and even perspiring. To achieve these results while awake, we would need to engage in a serious workout at the gym. However, during a dream, the mind can quickly take us through an elaborate set of experiences, emotions, and sensations as if they are actually happening. A nightmare can seem so real that we might feel terrified long after waking up, with the slightest noise in our home making us feel as if we are still in danger.

Several interesting questions arise after such an event: What caused my heart rate to increase? Why did my breathing become faster? What made me perspire? After all, we weren't in any real danger; we were comfortably tucked in our bed. The mind is so successful at creating false realities that its influence spreads throughout the body, tightening muscles and releasing stress hormones like cortisol that aid us in stressful situations.

In fact, as the primary stress hormone, cortisol increases sugars (glucose) in the bloodstream and enhances the brain's use of it, while increasing the availability of substances that repair tissues. Cortisol also curbs functions that would be nonessential or detrimental in a fight-or-flight situation and communicates with regions of the brain that control mood, motivation, and fear.

The long-term activation of this complex natural alarm system – and the subsequent overexposure to cortisol and other stress hormones – can disrupt almost all of the body's processes, putting us at an increased risk for numerous health problems, including:

- Anxiety
- Depression
- Digestive problems
- Headaches
- Heart disease
- Sleep issues
- Weight gain
- Memory and concentration impairment

This is why it's so important to learn healthy ways to cope with the stressors in our life. Ironically, few people in our lives emphasize the need for proper care of the mind.[1] Relatives, friends, athletic coaches, and medical practitioners place a lot of focus on maintaining physical health but rarely are we instructed to maintain and strengthen the mind.

Television shows and advertisements tell us to wear the right clothes, drive a nice car, have a nice home, and earn a lot of money. However, how useful are these things without proper mental health and well-being? We are a society that is expert at cleaning and polishing the birdcage but one that forgets to feed the bird.

## Illusions of the Mind

Lastly, our mind is a magician, taking small, insignificant thoughts and turning them into illusions of grandeur. How many times does the mind create a false reality? Much of what it conjures up isn't realistic or relevant and probably won't happen the way we imagine it will, making it especially important to evaluate the truth of our perception. If we don't give ourselves time to think things through, especially when it comes to the comments or actions of others, we can quickly let situations devolve in our minds. Before we know it, we will have thoroughly convinced ourselves that other people meant us harm.

---

[1] "Chronic Stress Puts Your Health at Risk," Mayo Clinic, April 21, 2016. https://www.mayoclinic.org/healthy-lifestyle/stress-management/in-depth/stress/art-20046037

A simple example of magically blowing things out of proportion is when we wave at a colleague and they do not respond. It is easy to jump to conclusions, taking offense and assuming they intentionally ignored us. The mind doesn't waste time in developing a narrative about this person and creates explanations as to why he or she doesn't like us and how they are being a jerk. We might even unfriend them on social media accounts. We can make an enemy out of this person when it's possible they just didn't see us waving at them.

Eastern wisdom suggests that this illusionist mind is our worst enemy, although through mindfulness it can become our best friend as it learns to recognize the tricks, stopping them before they go too far.

## Clearing the Traffic

According to *Psychology Today*, a person has an average of 25,000–50,000 thoughts every day. That's 1,000–2,000 thoughts each hour!

**Clearing the traffic jam in the mind**

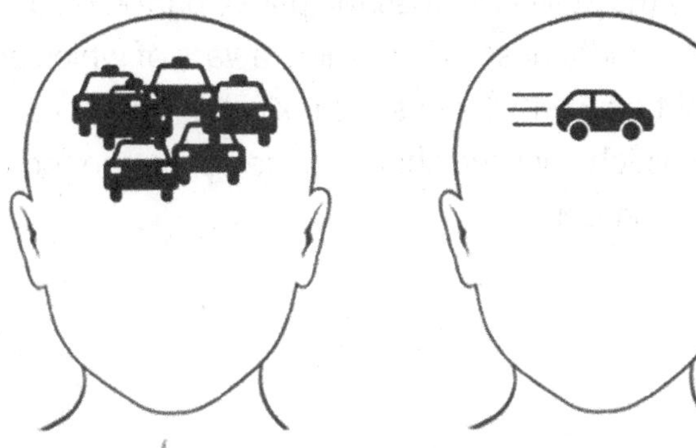

When I was living in the monastery on the Lower East Side of Manhattan, the noise from traffic and construction was unrelenting. However, I began to realize that the noisiest and busiest environment actually tended to exist in my mind. At the end of each day, we are left with a mental traffic jam comprised of thousands of ideas and impressions, creating noisy chatter that leaves us drained, exhausted, and distracted. Mindfulness can help clear the traffic jam so we can regain the level of clarity and focus required for the flow of innovation, peace, and tranquility.

Coming to terms with the idea that we have a mind similar to a runaway train can be humbling. We like the illusion of being in control of our outer environment, yet if we are not able to master what's happening on the inside, how can we control anything else? Managing our mind and emotions is a lot more difficult and challenging than controlling our external environment. It requires discipline, the willingness to take an honest look at ourselves, an openness to receiving feedback, and the readiness to correct and adjust our way of thinking, speaking, and behaving. Mindfulness allows us to not only become aware of our thought processes and patterns, but it also gives us the ability to press the pause button on our racing mind. Mindfulness is becoming aware of which apps are open right now, which ones are taking up our mental energy, and which ones we should close so we can focus on the present moment.

## Summary

- The mind, like a smart device, has many apps running in the background and if we don't learn to close out the apps we don't need, it will drain our battery, distract us, and prevent us from focusing.
- We have a tendency to dwell on and relive negative events from our past. The mind has a hard time letting go of such memories. The key is to catch ourselves as soon as this starts happening, stop that train of thought, and shift gears into something more positive.
- Replaying negative and stressful moments from the past or constantly worrying about the future can have a negative impact on our mental and physical health. What affects the mind also affects the body and vice versa.
- Mindfulness creates an awareness of the constant traffic jam that exists in the mind and enables us to clear out the traffic, so we can get to our destination without too many distractions.

## Reflection Questions and Exercises

Write down five to seven main things that are on your mind right now.

How are they impacting your emotions and behavior?

Analyze which of these thoughts or worries are not relevant to your life right now.

Once you have deciphered those thoughts or worries, try letting them go because they are irrelevant at the moment.

Identify and write down situations in your life that you are magnifying and blowing out of proportion and turning into a worst-case scenario.

Once identified, put the situation into perspective and ease your anxiety about it.

CHAPTER **FIVE**

# Mindfulness: What It Is and Isn't

## Overview

There are many misconceptions people have when it comes to mindfulness. This chapter addresses some of the misconceptions, such as: It's just for monks, and it can only be practiced sitting cross-legged.

With a basic understanding of how our mind works, we can move on to defining what mindfulness is, and, just as importantly, what it is not. It is all too common that when we come across advertisements for mindfulness and meditation, we see an attractive person wearing a yoga outfit, sitting cross-legged on a mat with their eyes closed, peacefully facing an ocean, mountain, or other serene landscape. This depiction leads to the conclusion that to engage in meditation, we must look and dress a certain way, while also being in nature.

Of course, situating oneself in a nonurban environment with minimal distractions can be extremely helpful. However, the reality is that most of our waking moments are spent in a busy office surrounded by colleagues, with a schedule packed with daily meetings, phone calls, and tasks. Afterward, we are stuck in an hour-plus commute via car or public transportation, and the moment we get home, family responsibilities await. If we spend more than half of our waking life in work-related responsibilities and personal obligations, who has time to sit in front of a mountain to meditate? Fortunately, mindfulness is much more accessible than how it is depicted in advertisements.

## It's Not How You Sit

Mindfulness isn't about sitting cross-legged on a yoga mat with your eyes closed, clearing your mind of all thoughts. No one needs to sit in a cross-legged position at all. Many people I come across at corporate workshops don't have the flexibility to sit in such a position, or they simply can't because of their required business attire. For most of my sessions, I have people sit in chairs, and make cushions and yoga mats available for those who prefer the floor. I tell people that I'd rather have them sit comfortably than being distracted by painful knees and ankles due to maintaining a difficult posture. The mind is already poised to wander, and there is no need to add additional distractions like challenging sitting positions.

## It's Not Just for Women

Women comprise 60–70% of my company conferences, retreats, or office meditations. A couple of days after writing this section, I led a meditation workshop for a health-based organization in Manhattan where 24 out of the 27 attendees were women. From my experience, because of their openness and eagerness to explore the inner self, it can be easier for women to dive right in and begin to evaluate their thoughts and emotions.

However, I hear positive feedback from many men who were initially hesitant because of some preconceived idea about what mindfulness is. Playing sports and working out in the gym are the stereotypical ways for men to work off stress and feel "like a man." Sitting peacefully, focusing on one's breath and becoming aware of one's emotions, just doesn't feel comfortable and might even seem a bit boring, but after hearing about the research and engaging in some practices, they have a change of heart and mind.

## It's Not Just for Passive Participants

It is common for people to believe that the relaxation from meditation will slow them down and be counterproductive in developing a competitive edge. After all, doesn't an athlete need to be aggressive to compete at the highest level?

In the past few years, professional athletes in the NBA and NFL have implemented meditation to improve performance during games and maintain composure when a referee's call doesn't go in their favor. NBA superstars like LeBron James, Kobe Bryant, and Michael Jordan have all used meditation and mindfulness techniques to take their game to the next level.[1] Olympic gold medalists Misty May-Trainor and Kerri Walsh have applied visualization and meditation to stay sharp on the volleyball court. Before his retirement, future baseball Hall-of-Famer Derek Jeter noted that an hour of morning meditation was a staple of his off-day routine. These athletes' success demonstrates the power of mental training, with plenty of science to back it up.[2]

---

[1]Johann Berlin, "How Athletes Stay Calm Under Pressure: Breath Is Everything," *Huffington Post*, January 1, 2017. https://www.huffingtonpost.com/johann-berlin/how-athletes-stay-calm-un_b_14179524.html

[2]Lisa Capretto, "Phil Jackson On Using Meditation And Mindfulness To Create Great Basketball Teams," *Huffington Post*, July 17, 2013. https://www.huffingtonpost.com/2013/07/17/phil-jackson-meditation-coaching-tactics_n_3606632.html

## It's Not Just for the Athletes

Phil Jackson won more NBA championships than any other coach, and he did it with more than one team. Mindfulness techniques were part of his training regimen while he coached the Chicago Bulls and Los Angeles Lakers. In an interview with Oprah, he explains, "I approached it with mindfulness. . . . As much as we pump iron and we run to build our strength up, we need to build our mental strength up . . . so we can focus . . . so we can be in concert with one another."[3]

Like any other muscle in our body, the brain must be exercised to remain strong and healthy. Otherwise, it will become weak and easily distracted, struggling to see the positive side of challenging situations. When the mind is easily overwhelmed, it becomes unnecessarily anxious about things that are unlikely to happen. The challenge of being in such high-profile positions, where millions of people are watching you on and off the court, and with popularity waxing and waning, is remaining composed throughout the season and not getting caught up in the sensational chatter of fans and media.

## It's Not Just for Sports

Professional coaches and athletes aren't the only ones using meditation to train their brains. The U.S. Army has employed various mindfulness practices to help soldiers deal with many unpredictable situations that they can encounter during active duty.

---

[3]Ibid.

Members of the Armed Forces face dangerous, high-performance, high-stress situations in active duty while leaving loved ones and the familiarity of home behind. These conditions can be overwhelming, and it is not enough for a soldier's physical body to be trained; it is also vital that the mind be fit and equipped with a "mental armor" of sorts.[4]

## It's Not Just About Breathing

Practicing mindfulness is not just about taking deep breaths to calm your anxiety and quell a racing mind.

## It's Not Just for Monks

Mindfulness and meditation are not only for monks who have renounced the world and isolated themselves from society to discover inner peace and happiness.

## It's for Everyone

**Mindfulness is for all walks of life.**

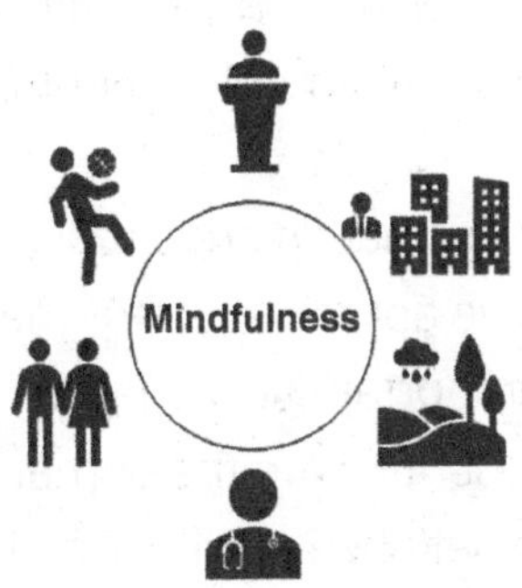


---

[4]Melissa Myers, "Improving Military Resilience Through Mindfulness Training," USAMRMC Public Affairs, June 1, 2015. https://www.army.mil/article/149615/improving_military_resilience_through_mindfulness_training

Meditative and mindful practices are for all of us. They are not only for folks who possess a calm and balanced demeanor, looking to achieve enlightenment and hoping for a spiritual or religious experience. The idea that mindfulness and meditation are only spiritual or religious rituals is a common misconception that can prevent people from experiencing the benefits of these practices. Although historically these tools have been used to achieve enlightenment and greater proximity to the divine, there is plenty of current research showing that a secular approach to mindfulness gives one a better understanding of their nature and behavior. These routines result in alertness and increased awareness to the triggers of our stress, anxiety, and fear, allowing a better understanding of the motivations behind our actions.

Through mindfulness, we can begin to question why we behave in certain ways. We may claim we only work to earn money, which pays the bills. However, other underlying factors may be more authentic motivators. Perhaps we are looking to prove something to ourselves or are hoping to outdo siblings, friends, or people we are competing with. We may be propelled by the desire to outperform others simply so we can feel good about ourselves and our accomplishments during the next family gathering.

These subconscious needs are a reality for many of us, and it's normal to crave appreciation for the good work we're doing. However, it's important to recognize whether competition and insecurities are the primary driving forces behind our efforts to get ahead in life. Can we work because we enjoy a job that gives us fulfillment? The more we can get in touch with our inner self, the more real and honest we can be with ourselves and others.

## Summary

- Mindfulness isn't just for monks and advanced yogis.
- It's not exclusively done for spiritual purposes. It can be practiced in a secular manner for the purpose of growth.
- It's for anyone and everyone who has a desire to raise their self-awareness and remain calm and focused during the roller coaster of life.
- Although helpful, it doesn't have to be practiced only in serene environments or in nature.

## Reflection Questions and Exercises

What are some misconceptions you have or have had about mindfulness?

How do you think practicing mindfulness can help you in your personal and professional life?

CHAPTER **SIX**

# The How, When, and Where of Mindfulness

## Overview

Mindfulness can be practiced just about anywhere: at home, in the office, in the car, at the park, while walking in the park, and even while eating. We have become so restless and addicted to our smart devices that we can hardly take a bite out of our food without checking our phone. Just as we take on a gym membership to get in shape or take driving lessons to learn to drive, we can meditate to learn how to operate the complex vehicle of the mind.

While there exists a large variety of mindfulness techniques, I have found the following to be most effective when teaching corporate professionals how to utilize meditation to manage their emotions, reduce stress, and improve their focus and productivity. All of these techniques are secular and have no religious connotations. They all do come from one of the Eastern traditions; however, what I teach isn't invoking any particular deity or chanting any mantras whatsoever. My own personal practice includes a combination of the secular and the spiritual. However, in corporate settings, it's all purely secular so as to not impose on anyone's belief system. For the most part, the practices involve a variety of breathing exercises that gradually bring the participants to a calm state of mind where they become aware of the thoughts, emotions, and stress they might be holding in. They are then guided through a set of practices to help improve their focus and concentration and feel grateful for the positive events that are currently happening in their lives.

## The Ideal Time

If you're a monk, the best time to meditate is around 4 a.m., well before the sun comes up. For the 15 years I lived as a monk, I was waking up between 4 a.m. and 5 a.m. daily. It wasn't always easy, but it was definitely worth it because it gave my mind a good workout before the day began. Early morning hours are recommended because there is little activity happening at that time of the day. The mind is a bit quieter as well, making it easier to focus.

However, for those of us who aren't monks, my recommendation is to start your day with a short meditation, even if it's just three to five minutes or even a minute. If you're not a morning person or if you have way too many responsibilities at home to take care of before running out the door, find a time during the day that works for you. It could be as soon as you get to the office, before your meeting. It could happen during your lunch break while sitting in your office or car or any decently quiet place. Perhaps there's a conference room at work that you could reserve and take out five minutes to close your eyes and dive in for a little meditation break. Such breaks can help us decompress, destress, release tension, and regain clarity and objectivity.

Meditating in the evening or right before going to sleep is also a great way to disconnect from the day's events and clear the mind for a good night's sleep. Make sure your phone is on "do not disturb," take a few deep breaths to clear your mind, and let the tension in your body release.

Ultimately, each person will need to decide on the time that best suits them for meditating based on convenience and schedule. It is more important that we focus on regularity and consistency, even if the days and times for meditation fluctuate.

## A Sustained Practice

There are varying opinions on the topic of how long one should meditate. Personally, I think it's not practical to prescribe a certain amount of time, simply because everyone is in a different space in their journey and has a specific capacity to engage in this kind of practice. I am also a firm believer in taking things slowly and gradually, as I feel that the result will be more sustainable if we take baby steps. Of course, there are some who can dive right in and have no problem committing to longer periods of time right from the get-go. However, from my experience, that is not the case for the vast majority.

My personal goal when I teach mindfulness practices is for people to be able to maintain the practice for the rest of their life, or at least a very extended period of time. The true benefits of a mindfulness meditation practice will manifest only for those who maintain a consistent engagement with it. By going to the gym just once, the only thing one really experiences is soreness and pain, but over a period of time, we notice our muscles becoming toned, we feel ourselves becoming stronger and healthier, and our stamina for practicing also increases.

When I used to lecture extensively on college campuses and teach students the different meditation practices, I remember that it was difficult for them to remain consistent with it even though I was recommending that they practice only 15 minutes per day. To put this in perspective, this equals about 1% of our entire day. I gradually reduced my recommendation to 10 minutes a day, and even that wasn't received with success. It's quite surprising and interesting that we spend 5 to 10 hours per day looking at screens, which includes scrolling through social media platforms, but we have a hard time spending 1% of our time on an activity that can literally help us with our depression, anxiety, and self-awareness.

Now that I'm speaking at corporations and conferences, I have gained a better understanding of the capacity people have for committing to a mind-strengthening practice. I encourage individuals to start with a three- to five-minute daily practice and try to do it every single day, which is increasingly more difficult for people to commit to – doing something every single day. I don't want people to feel like meditation is a burden, and I don't want people to feel guilty if they can't do it every single day. Sometimes what happens is if someone skips a few days, guilt kicks in and the practice is abandoned altogether. It is more valuable to meditate a few times a week than to not do it at all. I have chosen to take a lenient approach in terms of how much time I prescribe for the practice. We can even do it for short one-minute increments, several times a day, in between meetings and tasks.

I often tell my corporate audiences, because many of them are high achievers, goal setters, and very successful individuals, that there is no need for them to become a Type A meditator. That kind of approach to meditation will not work and a slow and gradual goal will bear more fruit in time. It's important to see this type of practice as a marathon and not a sprint; it's better to pace oneself and increase the practice in very small increments of one to two minutes after one has been able to successfully meditate for three to five minutes for the entire month. If one continues to add one to two minutes each month, one can reach 15 to 20 minutes by the end of the year and that will also serve as a great effort to build confidence in one's ability to prolong the practice.

## Finding Your Environment

### At Home

If it's possible to create a space in your home that is not overly cluttered and not too distracting, then that would be a more ideal environment for practicing meditation. As I mentioned earlier, the mind responds to the environment around us. It acts very much like a wet sponge which absorbs everything it comes across. If there is clutter all around, then our mind could be affected by it. It's also helpful to have a clean space where one can meditate, and of course if one can create the quiet space where there isn't too much sound, that would also be very helpful.

### Parks and Nature Trails

Obvious places outside of the home that could work well are parks and nature trails. These environments are naturally peaceful and free of distractions and as long as you don't mind the bugs that might crawl up your leg, then you should be fine.

### The Beach

The beach is great, and one can simply sit and listen to the waves crashing and feel the cooling breeze. It's not too difficult to clear the mind in this type of environment. Mornings or evening would be best for the beach because when it gets crowded, there are way too many sights and sounds for the mind to become peaceful.

### In the Car

If there's no possibility of using a conference room or office at work, then you can even sit in your car before stepping into the office and a take few quiet moments to get ready to tackle the challenges that await. Using your car to decompress in the middle of the day, during lunch, with some calming music playing in the background can also be very refreshing and relaxing. During a regular commute or if you find yourself stuck in traffic and worried about the meeting that you might be late to or even miss, you can easily start taking slow and deep breaths and keep your emotions calm while you get to your destination. Just make sure you don't close your eyes, duh!

### On the Bus and Train

If you don't drive to work and can't use your vehicle to meditate in, we can even engage in meditation, as unlikely as it may seem, while using public transportation such as the train or bus. The idea of meditating in an environment that is crammed with people and very stressful seems somewhat counterintuitive. However, if we can learn to close our eyes and think positive thoughts while in such a hectic space, meditating in a calmer environment is going to become a little easier. This kind of practice is also training our mind that it is possible to stay calm and relaxed during stressful situations that tend to cause us to become very tense. Using public transportation isn't the most recommended environment for meditating, but if we spend an extended amount of time commuting to and from work, then it's definitely a place that can be utilized to regain our composure either before getting to work or getting home to engage with our family and home responsibilities.

**Being mindful in any environment**

The point is, once we experience the benefits and become determined to do it, we will find ways to make it happen, just as we do with anything that we really want to do in life. There are dozens of ways and places we can meditate, and our mind will give us creative reasons and excuses and create obstacles telling us why we can't do it in this place or that place. However, we can either choose to listen to the mind or develop the strength and determination and move forward with what we know is going to be great for us.

Regardless of the environment, it would be great if for whatever amount of time that we're going to meditate, that we can put our smart devices away and put them on silent or airplane mode so we are not tempted to look at them when notifications are received. Our tremendous addiction to checking our phones every 30 seconds can hamper our ability to sit with a quiet mind.

## Posture

I am often asked if it is necessary for individuals to sit cross-legged while meditating. If I said yes to this question, then I would be very unfair to all those who have never sat cross-legged or are unable to sit in that type of position. When I teach mindfulness practices in corporations, I have everybody stay in their chairs and sit comfortably. If one wants to sit cross-legged, that is perfectly fine, but it is not mandatory. Sitting on a chair is totally fine. However, I don't recommend sitting on a couch or something that is overly comfortable, which might induce one to fall asleep. We do want to remain alert so that we can engage the mind in these various techniques and keep the mind active and of course that can't happen if we begin to fall asleep.

On many occasions, when I lead mindfulness sessions at companies, people end up dozing off even though they're sitting in conference room chairs surrounded by their colleagues. This is fairly normal because we all carry around a lot more fatigue than we're aware of. It's a good indicator of the amount of exhaustion we might be carrying around. The moment someone takes over and begins to guide a meditation practice, the mind begins to relax, and as a result, the body begins to relax and then the next natural thing to happen is to go to sleep. We don't need to feel guilty or embarrassed if we end up falling asleep during our meditation. It probably means we were so tired that we needed it and that the meditation is actually working because it was able to clear our mind and relax our body to such a degree that we begin to snooze. This means we need to get more sleep or better sleep. If we are meditating in the morning or at the office in the afternoon, the goal isn't to fall asleep. Rather, we're hoping to recharge our battery and regain some clarity, focus, and energy. To be able to do that, we need to try our best to not fall asleep. One way to do this is to keep our eyes slightly but not completely open because then we'll get distracted by all the objects around us. Keeping our eyes open just a few millimeters so that some light comes in but everything is blurry will prevent us from falling asleep and will also help us concentrate and keep the mind from wandering off too far.

## Enhancing Productivity

It may seem like a natural conclusion that meditation will calm and relax us to such a degree that we won't be as productive as we need to be to meet our goals and deadlines. However, I like to think of the meditation process as clearing the traffic jam in the mind. When we drive in heavy traffic during rush hour, it's hard to make much progress. We're just inching along because there are so many other vehicles on the road. If the traffic jam can be cleared, we would begin to make much more progress and could reach our destination at a faster pace. Similarly, meditation clears the traffic jam in our mind, which allows us to have a refreshed perspective and gives us the ability to think with increased clarity, allowing us to progress and achieve the things we need to achieve.

There is much research and published articles that show that the practice of mindfulness can boost productivity.[1] If a car engine overheats, it's not going to help us get to our destination faster. We need to stop the car, let the engine cool down, and then continue, which is exactly what meditation does for our mind, emotions, and body.

## Confronting Restlessness

**Juggling professional and personal lives**

[1]Peter Bregman, "If You're Too Busy to Meditate, Read This," *Harvard Business Review*, October 12, 2012. https://hbr.org/2012/10/if-youre-too-busy-to-meditate.html

"My mind is all over the place and I just can't sit and focus." I have heard this type of complaint hundreds of times and my response is, "Welcome to the club!" Most of us are juggling so many responsibilities between our work and our personal lives that we have made it almost impossible for the mind to be peaceful. At times it can feel like there is a hurricane of thoughts in our head and it's impossible to sit still while a storm is taking place. So, this is not a valid excuse or a reason to avoid practicing meditation. On the contrary, we need to meditate to help get rid of the stormy weather that is preventing us from being peaceful.

For many of us, we take on a gym membership because we're not fit and healthy. Likewise, we take driving lessons to learn how to handle a vehicle, which can help us get from one place to another. Similarly, we learn to meditate so we can manage the vehicle of the mind so it can help us get to the places we want to be and not get distracted by all the "exits" of life.

Sitting still is becoming increasingly challenging for all of us. Having hundreds of apps to keep us distracted and being able to check out our friends' and strangers' profiles with a quick touch of the screen can immediately whisk us away from our present reality and into someone else's. The mind is not satisfied with looking at one or two profiles. Rather, it needs to look at dozens of profiles, which often leads to either depression after we see all the fun others are having, or an unhealthy pleasure when we see their miseries. We have gotten ourselves addicted to our smart devices and just as every addiction can be dangerous, so is this one. It's gotten to such a point that we're even putting our lives at risk by checking our phones even while driving or crossing the street. According to the National Transportation Safety Board,

"Many drivers believe they can multitask and still operate a vehicle safely. But multitasking is a myth. Humans can only focus cognitive attention on one task at a time. That's why the driving task should be a driver's sole focus."[2]

It has become practically impossible for us to focus on and do only one activity at a time. Somehow, that doesn't provide enough excitement for our mind and therefore, we need to eat, text, video chat with a friend while watching our favorite show on Netflix – all at the same time. While it might feel good to be this busy and to be doing all of these activities simultaneously, it can make the mind very restless when we don't have a lot going on. We try and do a million things at once and work ourselves up into a frenzy and then suggest that it's too hard to meditate. It would be silly to feed a child a ton of sugary food items at night and then expect them to fall asleep. It would be very counterproductive.

**Do we love being distracted?**

[2]"Eliminate Distracted Driving," National Transportation Safety Board, updated December 23, 2022. https://www.ntsb.gov/Advocacy/mwl/Pages/mwl-21-22/mwl-hs-05.aspx

So, if this describes our situation, we definitely need to take the time to rebuild the stamina of the mind to focus on one thing. We have become the ultimate multitasking generation. For some, there's even a certain thrill when we juggle many tasks and get lots done. However, an article from the *Harvard Business Review* suggests that "efficiency can drop as much as by 40%" for those who multitask, that multitaskers do less and miss information, and that "multitasking does not exist." What we are actually doing is switching from one task to another. The fact that texting while driving has become a major cause of car accidents should be a good indicator that our mind can really only focus on one task at a time. It's better and more productive for us to finish one task completely before taking on a different one. It takes a certain amount of energy and time to resume an activity once it has been halted. It disturbs the flow of the work, and having to bring our attention back into the groove isn't easy. Of course, there are times when we need to stop one task, take a break, and then get back into it with a fresh and clear perspective. There's nothing wrong with that because we went as far as we could have and then intentionally switched.

## Using Apps

An increasingly common question is whether individuals should utilize apps to help them meditate. Using an app can definitely help facilitate the process. It's a lot easier if someone is guiding you through a practice so you're not having to think about what you're going to do next while you're in the process of meditating. If you only have a five-minute break between meetings and you really just need to clear your mind, the convenience of an app is something that may help, and since we already have a gazillion apps on our devices that distract the hell out of us, it makes sense to have other apps that help us declutter our mind and focus.

There are dozens of apps out there and new ones coming out all the time. One would need to try them out and see which one seems to be the right fit. Many have a free trial period that will give participants an opportunity to take a test drive and see how it feels. At some point, one might be able to develop their own personal routine where they no longer need an app.

## Music and Meditation

Whether one wants to have music playing in the background or would rather prefer a quiet environment is completely up to the individual. I don't feel there is one right way or wrong way to do this. For some, background sounds and music can be distracting while for others it can be useful and can facilitate the practice. If one is meditating in a noisy place it might be helpful to have some calming background sounds such as the rain or the ocean or some soothing music playing.

Music influences human emotions and behavior rather significantly. When we hear a song that we used to listen to in high school, it brings back many of the experiences and emotions we felt when we used to listen to that song. Whether we have good memories or painful ones associated with that particular song, they all come rushing back in an instant. Blues music will have a different effect on us than hip-hop, classical, or death metal. The point is to be conscious of the fact that the sounds that are entering our ears will influence us tremendously, so we must be thoughtful about music when we sit down to meditate and go about our regular day-to-day activities.

There are even some types of meditations that involve an audible recitation of sound vibrations known as mantras. Reciting a mantra over and over again allows the mind to center on the sound vibration of the mantra being verbalized. It gives the mind something specific to focus on. Most of the time, but not always, mantras can be more on the spiritual side and are used by practitioners to go deeper into their spiritual journey and understand their purpose in life. Probably the most popular and widely known mantra is the one-syllable Om, which many yoga teachers recite during the conclusion of their classes. As a monk, I learned a variety of meditation practices. Using mantras was and continues to be a large portion of what I personally practice. However, since mantras can be more spiritually oriented and I don't want anyone to feel uncomfortable, these are not included in my corporate sessions.

## Living in the Present

When we go on a relaxing walk, instead of looking at the sky, clouds, trees, or birds, we're often focused on our smart devices. This lack of mindfulness can be dangerous because many of us can't seem to wait until we've crossed the street before we look at our device. It's becoming increasingly difficult for us to do almost anything without constantly looking at our phones. A fun challenge I like to throw out to corporate professionals is that when you take a break in the middle of the workday, go for a short walk but leave your smart device behind and just observe the surroundings around you and allow your brain to decompress from all the digital inputs it's constantly receiving from the screens at work and on our personal devices. Whether you're walking in a park or a busy city environment, try to become aware of your surroundings as there might be things you might not have noticed in the past. Make it an intentional walk so you get some exercise, feel refreshed, and give your eyes a break before you go back to your desk and start staring at screens again.

In addition to distracted strolls, it's come to a point where we can hardly take a bite out of our food without flipping through our devices to check the news or social media. It's almost as if the meal won't be complete if we're not scrolling. I wonder if a phoneless meal is equivalent to eating food without salt; it just wouldn't taste the same. This habit has made its way to the dinner table even when we sit with our family.

Here's a meditation that I would like to suggest: Try and eat one meal a day without looking at your phone. Smell and taste the food, and if you're with your family, engage in a conversation and ask about their day. I don't suggest eating all three meals without our devices because I think that poses an insurmountable obstacle. I'm not sure if I can do that myself! So, let's start with one meal a day. Feel free to pick your shortest and quickest meal of the day without feeling like you're cheating. Be happy that you're at least starting with one and hopefully that will grow into two or even three.

## Summary

- In order for us to learn to operate a vehicle properly, we need training and regular practice. Similarly, meditation helps us manage the vehicle of the mind; however, it also requires some training and steady practice.
- We need to get rid of the excuse that "I can't meditate because my mind is too restless." This is like saying, "I'm too unhealthy to go to the gym." We go to the gym to become healthy, so we meditate to create calm within the mind.
- It may feel good to try and multitask; however, research shows that multitasking reduces efficiency by 40%. The mind switches tasks and can't do two things at once. If it could, texting while driving wouldn't be prohibited.

## Reflection Questions and Exercises

Too often people feel that they don't have time to meditate. The following writing exercise will help strategize how, when, and where to start and maintain a meditation practice. Please use the following table for this exercise.

What are the best times of the day for you to engage in a mindfulness meditation practice? It doesn't have to be the same time each day. The time for each can be different. It's okay if some days are left blank.

What would be the ideal length of time you would like to start with? Better to start off slow than try and go all out right away. It can be as little as three minutes.

Identify the ideal locations that would be most conducive to practicing mindfulness meditation. Visualize your ideal setting and try and create that space.

| Day | Time of Day | Length of Time in Minutes | Location for Each Session |
|---|---|---|---|
| Monday | | | |
| Tuesday | | | |
| Wednesday | | | |
| Thursday | | | |
| Friday | | | |
| Saturday | | | |
| Sunday | | | |

CHAPTER **SEVEN**

# Mindful Awareness in Leadership

## Overview

What is a mindful leader and what can one do to become one? It requires introspection and self-awareness and honestly analyzing our motivations behind wanting to be in a leadership role. This chapter describes some highly successful individuals who fall into this category and set a proper example of what it means to become a mindful leader.

In this chapter, a theoretical framework for developing mindful leadership is also presented. This framework is rooted in a thorough understanding of the concepts, a desire to acknowledge and understand one's own nature and shortcomings, and a consistent application of the practices. Without all three components, the development will remain incomplete. This process enables empathic and compassionate behavior which is crucial for healthy leadership.

Mahatma Gandhi's quote "Be the change you want to see in the world" is a perfect example of what it takes to be a mindful and conscious leader. It puts the onus on one's self. If we want others to act and behave differently, we have to implement the change in ourselves first. Asking others to change while we stagnate in our character and habits is not only ineffective, but it is also unrealistic and hypocritical, quickly eroding trust and creating resentment.

Change is hard and most of us don't look forward to it. How many times have we tried to part ways with a bad habit that we're not so proud of, only to fall back into those tendencies? How many New Year's resolutions for eating healthier, exercising, saving more money, or having better relationships have we committed to, only to lose our determination one week later?

Change is also not something that manifests overnight. We have to work for months or even years to be the change we want to see in the world. Change requires patience and time, and if we can understand this, we will save ourselves much frustration and heartache.

Mindfulness provides the means through which we can develop this greater level of patience. It's the act of becoming aware of our thoughts, feelings, desires, and emotions, and bringing the distracted mind back to the present moment. This in-the-moment awareness is so important because too often we keep pushing through our day, never stopping to think about our emotions and how we are being influenced by them. With each negative and difficult exchange, we add additional baggage on our already weighed down mind, which not only adds stress to our lives but also clouds our judgment and ability to empathize. Through mindful awareness, we can avoid, prevent, or lessen the unpleasant impacts from our emotional reactions toward others and change our habits.

## Motivation for Leading

How is this awareness important and relevant to taking on a leadership role? Mindful leadership is about asking ourselves what the real motivation is for taking a particular role or performing a specific action. What is the motivation for taking up a leadership position? Do we want to serve others, or are we more interested in being served? Is it attractive to be in control of everyone, or are we interested in helping others grow and thrive? When we walk into a room, do we spread inspiration or instill fear?

Too often, people will go into a leadership role for the wrong reasons, such as money, power, fame, and the ability to control people and resources. When this happens, the spirit of servant-leadership is forgotten. Self-aggrandizement then becomes the prominent goal while the interest of the organization and the workforce become secondary. If we're chasing fame and glory, only looking out for ourselves, this behavior creates a toxic "every man for himself" atmosphere that will not be sustainable. Leadership can bring about several perks, but they are meant to be utilized in the service of others. Mindful leadership is regularly asking ourselves what we need to do to become better individuals and leaders at work, at home, and in our communities.

## Leading by Example

One of the key traits of a mindful leader is leading by example. We are tired of being told what to do by leaders who aren't following their own advice. This hypocrisy is a huge turnoff and deteriorates trust in the leadership, making it crucial that those in a leadership position follow through on the advice they give to others. Leaders can provide tremendous inspiration by simply doing the things they are asking others to do, which also helps them stay connected and relevant to the workforce. Gandhi and Martin Luther King Jr. are great examples of this. They led their freedom marches personally. They didn't sit back comfortably and make others do all the heavy lifting and dangerous work. These mindful leaders knew that if they weren't out on the front lines, people would lose the passion to bring about great change. Because these leaders led by example, showing immense courage and compassion, they inspired the entire planet! It's so important for us as leaders to be visible to our workforce and communities. We have to personally demonstrate that there is no gap between the leader and the people we lead.

That's the difference between a boss and a leader. A boss is in the back, ordering everyone else to charge ahead; a leader is on the front line, helping everyone push forward together. We need to constantly ask ourselves which model we are following. There may be times where a little of both is required.

### Haruka Nishimatsu

Haruka Nishimatsu, a former CEO of Japan Airlines, had a very nontraditional approach to his leadership model. He led by example and tried his best to be the leader, not the boss.

He wasn't aspiring to be the most important person in the room, which was demonstrated when he tore down his office and began sitting in the open space shared by his co-workers. During lunch, he got in line with everyone else and sat and ate lunch with the rest of the staff. Nishimatsu wanted to be accessible and relatable to his employees, who could approach him and share ideas. He didn't want to create a barrier between himself and the rest of the workforce.
At times, he would walk into airplanes, talk to the flight attendants, and even help arrange newspapers. Nishimatsu didn't want to be in his office behind closed doors, far removed from the experience of the rest of the employees; he wanted to share in it. Once, when the airline was not doing well, causing the need for pay cuts, Nishimatsu cut his pay as well. How many of us would be willing to do that? We can only imagine the kind of respect he earned from his employees through the mindful leadership he adopted.

**Tim Duncan**

Another great leadership example is NBA Hall of Fame San Antonio Spurs basketball player Tim Duncan. Out of the 19 years that he played the sport before retiring, Tim was chosen for the all-star team 15 times. More impressive is that he stayed with the same organization for 19 years. That kind of loyalty is becoming increasingly rare in this day and age. Even rarer, later in his career, to bring in younger and fresher players, Tim cut his annual salary by $10 million to benefit the rest of the team. Imagine, in your own lives and work, being willing to give up such a significant portion of your salary for the benefit of someone else. A real leader should be able and willing to make this kind of sacrifice and put the interest of the organization ahead of their own. Most people would be easily swayed by greed and just keep the extra money whether needed or not. Putting others' needs before our own can be difficult but is an essential ingredient to authentic mindful leadership.

### The Humble Monk

The first time I had a chance to personally witness someone leading by example was when I had decided to spend time in a monastery in Mumbai, formerly known as Bombay, India. The meditation practices started at 5 a.m. sharp and all the monks were required to be there on time. Since I was a guest, there were no such expectations placed on me, but I wanted to be part of the program and not look like a slacker. Therefore, I made sure to be on time every day.

Before the morning services began, a few monks cleaned the entire floor of the meditation hall. They first used an Indian broom, which had a short stick attached to it, requiring one monk to squat or bend over while sweeping the floor. No easy task by any means! After sweeping, they mopped with a simple floor rag and a bucket of water to dunk the dirty cloth in, rinse and repeat. When finished, all the ceiling fans would be turned on high to dry off the floor.

I naturally assumed that those assigned to cleaning the floors were the newer, inexperienced monks-in-training. Why else would they be doing the menial work of cleaning floors? However, while I was attending a daily study session for the resident monks, to my surprise, I noticed that the teacher and main speaker for the session was one of the monks who had cleaned the floor. Some days later, I noticed the same monk in the kitchen, helping cook for the monks and visitors. When he wasn't cooking and cleaning, he would deliver powerful and inspirational lectures during the Sunday program, which were attended by thousands of people.

What really impressed me was that he was equally enthusiastic in all of his services, and he didn't treat one task as being better than another. He was the senior monk and knew that others, particularly younger monks, would observe his behavior and most likely adopt his mood and attitude. This leader knew that to set the right example, he needed to show there was no shame in doing menial tasks, and that all services should be seen as a privilege.

It's very common for individuals within a community or a company to compare themselves with others. The natural outcome is that we end up seeing all of our amazing qualities while noticing the deficiencies in others. With everyone in the monastery required to do menial service regardless of rank and social status, the individuals in this group were forced to see themselves as the servant of everyone else, preventing anyone from thinking they were better than anyone else.

## Walking the Talk

Even though the environment of a fast-paced, profit-centered corporation might be the polar opposite of a humble monastery, leaders in corporations can learn valuable lessons from these monks, who were very educated and capable yet perfectly demonstrated the principle of servant leadership. The monks understood that the future generation would follow in their footsteps and knew it was their duty to act in a way that inspired proper behavior and culture. To hope for an environment of cooperation and trust, mindful leaders know they must engage in the same activities like the other residents.

Due to this very down-to-earth demeanor, the monks not only inspired the younger residents but also the thousands of congregation members who would regularly attend the programs. During my short stay at the monastery, I learned that many of the congregants were very wealthy and influential, with some ranking among the top entrepreneurs in all of India. Yet, when they came to the monastery, they were never given preferential treatment. Attendees could be seen cooking in the kitchen and meditating sitting on the floor with everyone else. These people who moved in prestigious circles in society were encouraged to see themselves as servants to the rest of the attendees at the monastery.

Society, as we have come to know it, places value on those who have money and prestige, but wouldn't it be a refreshing sight if those in power could develop the spirit of serving others and remaining humble amid their success? Wouldn't it be wonderful if CEOs, politicians, supervisors, and managers understood themselves to be the servants of those below them as opposed to trying to micromanage and control them? How amazing would it be if those in power made it their main priority to uplift and inspire others instead of feeling threatened by their progress and thereby discouraging them or pushing them down? We generally treat others the way we are treated. Doesn't it make sense, then, to treat everyone else the way we would like to be treated? We like to talk about servant leadership, but the reality is that it's quite difficult to execute. Power is intoxicating. It inflates our ego. Some love the feeling of being able to tell others what to do.

## Humility in Leadership

The humble appearance of mindful leadership may seem to lack the strength and fire of confidence and passion. It may seem like a humble individual will not be able to earn the respect of their peers. However, there is a deeper understanding of what the mantle of humility is. According to an article in *Forbes*, "a humble leader is secure enough to recognize his or her weaknesses and to seek the input and talents of others."[1] To be humble is to realize, with some sense of relief, that we don't always have to have the right answer, and that we can, and should, seek the help of others. A humble leader has learned that it is not a sign of insecurity or weakness to ask for support. According to Ken Blanchard, author of *The One Minute Manager*, humble leaders "don't think less of themselves, they just think of themselves less."[2]

---

[1]Doug Guthrie, "The Paradox Of Humility In American Business And Society," Forbes, November 15, 2013. https://www.forbes.com/sites/dougguthrie/2013/11/15/the-paradox-of-humility-in-american-business-and-society/?sh=79f6086b7b7a

[2]Rodger Dean Duncan, "Ken Blanchard: Why Servant Leadership Requires Humility," *Forbes*, May 8, 2019. https://www.forbes.com/sites/rodgerdeanduncan/2019/05/08/ken-blanchard-why-servant-leadership-requires-humility/?sh=4ad7cc4625f2

The paradigm of leadership, whether in corporations or politics, needs to change if we hope to see any kind of change in society. This change isn't going to be easy and, as Gandhi stated, it has to start with one's self; it will require humility and rely on a mindset of service. Martin Luther King Jr. said in his "Drum Major Instinct" sermon, "If you want to be important – wonderful. If you want to be recognized – wonderful. If you want to be great – wonderful. But recognize that he who is greatest among you shall be your servant."

## Summary

- Mindfulness in leadership can help leaders become aware of their motivations for being in a leadership role and come to a point where leading to serve can become their primary inspiration.
- Leading by example is the only true way to inspire others and the former CEO of Japan Airlines, Haruka

Nishimatsu, demonstrated this by giving himself a pay cut when the rest of the workforce was asked to do the same.

- Tim Duncan, former star of the San Antonio Spurs, put the interest of his team ahead of his own by sacrificing part of his income for the future success of his team.
- Humility in leadership should not be seen as a weakness. Asking for help and acknowledging one's shortcomings takes courage, vulnerability, and strength, all traits of a confident leader.

## Reflection Questions and Exercises

The following questions need to be answered with complete honesty and after some thoughtful reflection. They are meant to help develop a greater level of self-awareness.

What were your initial motivations for wanting to be in a leadership position?

________________________________________

________________________________________

________________________________________

________________________________________

How have your motivations changed over time?

________________________________________

________________________________________

________________________________________

________________________________________

Do you feel that you were, or are now, influenced to lead by the desire to have power, influence, fame, and control?

______________________________________________

______________________________________________

______________________________________________

______________________________________________

How much of your motivation to lead is coming from a desire to serve, encourage, and helping people grow?

______________________________________________

______________________________________________

______________________________________________

______________________________________________

During your time as a leader, have you, due to some unconscious biases, suppressed another employee's opinion or growth?

Identify the individuals you suppressed.

______________________________________________

______________________________________________

______________________________________________

______________________________________________

What was it about them that drove you to act in that way?

Is there anything you can do to rectify such past actions?

Do you lead by example? Do you do the things you ask others to do?

What are three things you can do in your organization to lead by example?

CHAPTER **EIGHT**

# Creating a Positive and Sustainable Workplace Culture

## Overview

Appreciating the contributions of our colleagues and co-workers and not feeling envious of their success are key components of developing a mindful workplace culture. This means that we intentionally take time to appreciate the contributions of others and communicate in a way that inspires and encourages them in their endeavors.

## The Value of Appreciation and Recognition

An incredibly important component of creating a mindful workplace culture is appreciation and recognition. We all know how it feels to work overtime on a project, working weekends to meet deadlines, only to have the project reach completion with no offers of recognition. This lack of appreciation leaves us deflated, uninspired, and unmotivated. If this response becomes the modus operandi of an organization, it will foster an environment in which employees won't put their hearts into the next project. Staff will begin to deliver the bare minimum, spend more time watching the clock, and might even put more effort into submitting resumes on LinkedIn.

If one is in a leadership role, it is vital to appreciate the workforce. Providing a paycheck is good but it's not always good enough. People need to know that leaders value their work and a personal gesture of appreciation can go a long way in developing and growing that relationship. Appreciation doesn't need to be a grand and expensive affair, and it doesn't always need to involve giving bonuses. Smaller gestures, like a genuine thank you for something specific, can be just as meaningful. People like to know the particular achievements you are appreciating them for, as it shows you're paying attention and are aware of their contributions. Providing lunch, or a day off, for the team that put in the extra effort to lead a project to success is another great way to express gratitude. Additionally, publicly appreciating someone's contributions in a company newsletter is a grander gesture because now not only you but the entire group or company is being made aware of the efforts of that employee.

An article published by *Harvard Health Publications* describes a study conducted by researchers from Wharton where they divided up fundraisers into two groups at the University of Pennsylvania.[1] One group made fundraising calls to "solicit alumni donations" as they had done in the past. The second group made their calls on a different day but received a "pep-talk from the director of annual giving," who expressed appreciation for their efforts. The group that received the call from the director made 50% more calls than the first group. Research like this shows how a simple and inexpensive formula greatly increases productivity in the workplace. It is surprising more companies aren't implementing this culture of appreciation into their organizations.

To further highlight the value of appreciation, research from the Society of Human Resources Management (SHRM) shows that it can cost a company six to nine months of an employee's annual income to find and train a new person.[2] This means to replace an employee who earned $50,000 a year, a company will spend approximately $25,000 to $37,500 to hire and train a new worker. Moreover, when a team member leaves, their absence affects morale and increases the workload and stress on their co-workers who now take on additional responsibilities and divert attention from their work.

Sheldon Yeller, the CEO of BELFOR Holdings, "a billion-dollar disaster relief and property restoration company," has

---

[1]Michael Craig Miller, "In Praise of Gratitude," *Harvard Health Publications*, November 21, 2012 (updated June 5, 2019). https://www.health.harvard.edu/blog/in-praise-of-gratitude-201211215561

[2]iGrad Author, "The Cost of Replacing an Employee and the Role of Financial Wellness," Enrich Financial Wellness. https://bit.ly/2xbSUPS

been handwriting a birthday card to each of his 8,000 employees since 1985.[3] He claims that this act has "made for a more compassionate, gracious workplace . . . since it makes people feel appreciated." For his 60th birthday, Yeller received 8,000 birthday cards from each of the employees. Yeller's long-time executive assistant says, "It really is an amazing tradition for a company our size. The cards always include a personalized note or memory shared, demonstrating how much Sheldon personally cares about every employee." According to the *Harvard Business Review*, positive social connections at work produce highly desirable results.[4] People get sick less often, experience less sense of depression, learn skills faster, remember important things longer, display better mental acuity, and simply perform better on the job. If people are happier, they are more productive.

Appreciation and recognition strengthen relationships and, simply put, people will do more when they are cared for. Relationships begin to break down when we start taking each other for granted and stop noticing the sacrifices we make for each other. Every human wants to know that their contributions mean something to others, and that they are adding value to the world around them. It's easy for us to remember when our leader or manager appreciated our efforts and congratulated us for a job well done; it makes us

---

[3]Chris Weller, "A CEO Who Writes 8,000 Employee Birthday Cards a Year Just Got the Ultimate 'Thank You,'" *Business Insider*, January 18, 2018. https://bit.ly/2N5bBQj

[4]Emma Seppälä and Kim Cameron, "Proof That Positive Work Cultures Are More Productive," *Harvard Business Review*, December 1, 2015. https://hbr.org/2015/12/proof-that-positive-work-cultures-are-more-productive

feel valued and part of the team. We replay that appreciation over and over again in our head because it brightens our day.

In this culture of appreciation, everyone's success is celebrated. When our working or social environments are too rooted in competition, then we are not eager to see others succeed. We can become "happy" when others fail. We do not want to cultivate a culture where we are unhappy to see others succeed and happy to see others fail. If we have a culture where we appreciate each other and celebrate each other's success, this will create harmony and a much stronger level of teamwork.

We have a human need to be appreciated, making it important to reflect on how often we appreciate others. When was the last time you appreciated a colleague, a friend, or a family member? Do you often expect them to appreciate you? How can we become better at appreciating others? These are some questions we all need to ask ourselves because appreciation is a two-way street.

Stronger teamwork emerges when we support and encourage one another. There is a wonderful example of strong teamwork from the natural world. The beautiful redwood trees of California, despite being so very tall, actually have very shallow roots. How do they survive all of the storms and natural challenges they face? It is because each tree's roots embrace the roots of their neighboring trees. There is an entire network of redwoods holding on to each other. They can weather any kind of storm together. If we learn to hold on to each other and support one another, everyone can succeed together.

## The Importance of Mindful Communication

One of the many amazing teachings I learned while living as a monk was the idea of being mindful of our communication. This was incredibly practical while living in a communal setting in a tiny three-bedroom Manhattan apartment where conflicts and disagreements can easily arise. You may be wondering, how is it possible for a bunch of peaceful monks to have disagreements and conflicts? It's important to keep in mind that when you have about a dozen grown men, all from very different cultural backgrounds, living and sharing a kitchen, bathroom, meditation space, study room, and floor space, it's easy for a little friction to take place. Moreover, just how peaceful can anyone be living on the Lower East Side of New York City where everyone is moving a hundred miles an hour trying to achieve success?

Conflicts are going to exist everywhere, whether it's a corporation, a family, a church, or a monastery. There's no avoiding that. The important thing is knowing how we're going to deal with it when it does arise. In the monastery, when a conflict or misunderstanding did occur, we were encouraged to be the first to approach our fellow monk and acknowledge that there was tension between us and, with humility, ask the question, "Can you please tell me what I did to contribute to the conflict?" The point wasn't to blame the other, because blame only brings about a reactive accusation from the other party. Since it takes two sticks to create a spark, we were encouraged to analyze what our role might have been to generate the conflict. Once we become aware of our contribution, it makes it much easier to approach the other from a place of humility. From my experience, every time I approached another in this spirit, it completely disarmed them and allowed for a healthy and productive discussion to take place, usually concluding with a nice big hug and a renewed and refreshed friendship.

Due to the proximity in which we all lived, we needed to practice this regularly. In a corporation, at the end of the day, you get to get away from your colleagues and go home, and you probably won't see those colleagues for another 12 hours. However, in a monastery, we don't go home because that is our home, our place of meditation and prayer and, in many regards, our workplace. We sleep within five feet of each other, meditate sitting in the same meditation room, and often cook together or are scheduled to engage in other services together. If there's an unresolved conflict, everything becomes difficult. There's little to no opportunity to create distance or to take a break. So, the only option for us was to resolve the conflict for our mental health, and for the entire environment. Conflict is never just between two people; everyone in the vicinity picks up on the cold war taking place.

Being the first to approach resolution with another is challenging for the ego because it's really hard to see our fault in the picture. Ego shows us what others do wrong and doesn't like to look in the mirror. By adopting this practice of forgiveness, we learn to tame our ego and allow ourselves to honestly see how we contributed to the friction that took place. This level of humility is crucial to implement in all components of our life and very applicable to corporate and workplace settings. With everyone racing around, multitasking and trying to meet deadlines, conflicts and disagreements are very natural. We shouldn't be surprised when conflicts take place – we should be surprised if they don't.

During my time as a monk, I learned about four important criteria to consider if we hope to make our communication as mindful as possible. It's not easy or possible to meet these criteria in all situations and at all times, however, if we take short moments to consider them, it will transform us into very thoughtful human beings.

### 1. Is It Truthful?

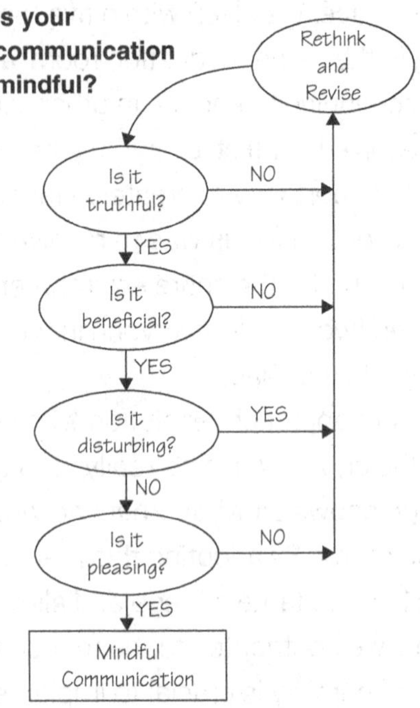


We should be able to analyze whether what we're about to say is factual; otherwise, we lose credibility and risk ruining a relationship. If we harbor some ill feelings toward an individual or have had some past conflicts with them, is it possible that we might not present all of the facts, or alter them to make that person look incompetent or untrustworthy? We need to be able to step back, look within, and assess whether we can be impartial. If we cannot interact equitably, there is a chance that we will not be as truthful as we need to be.

### 2. Is It Beneficial?

Ask yourself if what you are about to say will benefit the person and the situation or will make things worse. Even if your message meets the first criterion of being truthful, it is very important to consider whether it will meet the second criterion. In the heat of the moment, when there is a thunderstorm of emotions taking place inside us, it is going to be impossible for us to get our message across in a beneficial way. The truth can hurt and can come across as insensitive and harsh. Is what I am about to say going to hurt the other person? Of course, as we analyze our motives, we should ask ourselves if we intend to hurt the other person as a way of getting back at them for something. Are we convincing ourselves that we are helping when we are harming? Some reflection and self-awareness are required so that we do not falsely convince ourselves that something is beneficial.

### 3. Will It Disturb Them?

Ask yourself if what you are about to say is going to disturb and frustrate the other. If the answer is yes and if you're in a leadership role within your organization, it's important to consider the impact your words can have and what kind of mindset the communication will put the other person in. If the communication hasn't been thought out and ends up angering, scaring, or injuring someone's psyche, you can be sure it's going to have a negative impact on their productivity and increase the chances of mistakes being made – not to mention that it could end up demotivating and discouraging and lead to diminished loyalty toward you and the company.

### 4. Can I Communicate in a Pleasing Manner?

Last but not least, on a fundamental level, we should try our best to communicate in a manner that is pleasing to those we are speaking with, even if this communication is a kind of constructive criticism. Just try and imagine what it would do to your relationships, both personal and professional, if the communication we send out could be pleasing. After all, who doesn't want to receive positive messages?

Chances are, when we received positive messages, compliments, or appreciation, these communications made our day, and we can do the same for others.

As human beings, we go through a variety of emotions and day-to-day challenges that make it difficult to always be a mindful communicator. However, just getting into the habit of thinking about our written and verbal messaging can train us to be more mindful in every other aspect of our life.

## The Usefulness of Constructive Criticism

Those in leadership roles are often required to provide feedback and constructive criticism, which might come across as negative. Most of us don't like receiving feedback because it irks the ego. We take pride in the work we've done and don't want to see someone else dissect it and highlight the weak points. Of course, feedback can't be avoided and is necessary to ensure that things are done according to expectations. However, the key aspect is how that feedback is delivered and whether or not it was provided with sensitivity. Feedback and appreciation can be seen as the deposit and withdrawal columns on a bank statement, and, as with any bank account, it would be prudent to have more deposits than withdrawals.

If you're in a leadership or supervisory position and are about to provide feedback to an employee, it is crucial to evaluate the emotional bank account you have with that individual and then decide if it's wise to provide the feedback you're about to give. If your recognition of them isn't significantly outweighing the constructive criticism, you run a very high risk of draining that account and possibly even closing it. When that happens, whatever messages you hope to impart probably won't be heard with an open mind because the other person's perception is that you only see their shortcomings. Most likely, that person already has one foot out the door and has probably contacted recruiters looking for other opportunities. If we offer appreciation instead, a person will be able to hear our feedback more clearly and effectively.

It's impossible to be a good and mindful leader without being a good communicator. Real communication is all about listening; it is a dialogue, not a monologue. We should not be so forceful to change other people's opinions and positions before we have taken time to listen to them and understand why they think and feel the way they do. We always get so defensive when someone disagrees with us because it hurts our ego. Instead, we can always try to take a moment, take a breath, and hear what our colleague or friend is trying to say to us. They may have a very important message they are trying to convey. If we don't listen to them, we may miss what is hidden between the lines, and what is not being said. Are we paying attention to their facial expressions? Are we trying to understand their body language? We have to replace ego with empathy. We have to be able to put ourselves in the other person's shoes.

Here is a simple communication formula for you: Nature brilliantly designed us with two ears and one mouth. Sometimes I try to imagine what would have happened if it was the other way around, where we had two mouths and one ear. One mouth has gotten us into enough trouble! If we can remember this two-and-one formula and learn to use our ears twice as much we use our mouth, most of our relationships would experience a boost. Nature also kept our ears open and our mouths closed. No effort is needed to open our ears, but we need to work to open our mouth and speak. Nature is providing us an ideal approach to communication; we just need to take the time to learn it.

## Maintaining an Emotional Balance

Balanced emotions are another essential component of mindful communication, leadership, and culture. We all know what happens when we lose our cool. Our intelligence shuts off, and we make terrible mistakes that hurt and endure. We may even permanently destroy relationships. Anger is an emotion that can make us say and do things we deeply regret. We've all experienced this. Even in common communication like receiving a critical email from a colleague, we become very sensitive, and the next thing we know we're pounding out a harsh reply. When we are upset is precisely the wrong time to send a message, especially with instant communication models like email or texting so readily available. We must let ourselves cool off so we can regain our sense of balance, objectivity, and mindfulness.

In fact, this cooling-off period can change the region of our brain associated with self-regulation. As detailed in the *Harvard Business Review*, the anterior cingulate cortex, which sits behind our frontal lobe, helps us to plan and think with a long-term mindset.[5] This cortex allows us to shift our strategic responses and limits knee-jerk reactions like the angry email reply mentioned earlier. People who have suffered damage in this area of the brain show higher levels of impulsivity and unchecked aggression, but when they meditate regularly, they have demonstrated better results on psychological tests measuring self-regulation, and improvement in resisting distractions.

Mark Bertolini, the CEO of Aetna, introduced yoga and meditation into the workplace after recovering from a near-death experience he had from a bad skiing accident. Bertolini found that these mindful activities were incredibly helpful in his healing process, as they reduced the pain of his injuries and helped refocus his body and mind after such a traumatic

---

[5]Christina Congleton, Britta K. Hölzel, and Sara W. Lazar, "Mindfulness Can Literally Change Your Brain," *Harvard Business Review*, January 8, 2015.

episode. It was reported in the *New York Times* that 13,000 Aetna employees had participated in the yoga and meditation practices and they reported a 28 percent reduction in stress levels, a 20 percent improvement in sleep quality, and a productivity gain of 62 minutes per week, per employee.[6]

## Summary

- A paycheck is good, but it's not good enough.
- To keep the workforce enthused, inspired, and loyal, it is absolutely critical to regularly express appreciation for their endeavors.
- Sheldon Yellen, the CEO of BELFOR Holdings, handwrites almost 8,000 birthday cards to show his appreciation to his employees.
- If you want to be a good leader, you have to be a good communicator.
- It's important to consider if the communication you're about to send out is not only truthful and beneficial for the situation, but also whether it will end up disturbing the individual receiving the message.
- Finally, let's try and compose or deliver the message in a way that is pleasing and encouraging.
- We have been given two ears and one mouth so we can try to listen twice as much as we speak. Our ears are naturally open while an endeavor is required to activate the mouth.

---

[6]David Gelles, "At Aetna, a C.E.O.'s Management by Mantra," *New York Times*, February 27, 2015.

## Reflection Questions and Exercises

The following questions are meant to help you get in touch with how you feel when people in your professional and personal lives neglect you and how others are impacted by your behavior.

***Appreciation***

How does it feel when you are not appreciated for something you have put a significant amount of effort toward?

________________________________________

________________________________________

________________________________________

________________________________________

How does it affect your relationship with the person who didn't offer the appreciation you were expecting?

________________________________________

________________________________________

________________________________________

________________________________________

How will not being appreciated impact your mood and attitude toward future projects assigned to you by that individual?

________________________________________

________________________________________

________________________________________

________________________________________

How does it feel when you are appreciated for work you've done even if you weren't expecting appreciation?

How does it impact your relationship with the individual who expressed the appreciation?

How often do you appreciate your colleagues or workforce?

What can you do more of to show that you value them and what they bring to the table?

### *Communication*

The following exercise will help put you in the shoes of a person you might have communicated with in a way that was less than ideal and enables you to understand what goes through someone's mind and emotions when abrupt and unpleasant messages are communicated.

Remember a time when you received communication that seemed insensitive or unfair and ask yourself the following questions:

What are all the ways that communication made you feel?

________________________________________

________________________________________

________________________________________

________________________________________

How did this communication affect your relationship with that individual?

________________________________________

________________________________________

________________________________________

________________________________________

Did the individual do anything to rectify or apologize for the communication?

________________________________________

________________________________________

________________________________________

________________________________________

How many times did you end up remembering and recalling that incident?

______________________________________________

______________________________________________

______________________________________________

______________________________________________

Are you still bothered by this communication to this day?

______________________________________________

______________________________________________

______________________________________________

______________________________________________

***Now, take a moment to think about the following:***
When was the last time you received positive and pleasing communication?

______________________________________________

______________________________________________

______________________________________________

______________________________________________

How did this communication make you feel?

______________________________________________

______________________________________________

______________________________________________

______________________________________________

What are the ways in which the communication impacted your relationship with the sender?

________________________________________

________________________________________

________________________________________

________________________________________

What are some things you can do to ensure that your communication is more sensitive and mindful?

________________________________________

________________________________________

________________________________________

________________________________________

CHAPTER **NINE**

# Best Practices

## Overview

If we are looking to take a deeper dive for the purpose of understanding and analyzing why we do the things we do, what factors cause us to react and respond in certain ways, or how we can engage with the world while recognizing unconscious biases, then we will require consistency and commitment. It's important to understand that progress isn't always perceivable. Growth isn't always visible to us, but it is happening as long as we are following the process in a healthy and positive manner.

There are a variety of meditation practices in existence, so I like to take the time to explain the specific practices I engage in, along with the techniques I teach at corporate events. The practices I describe are secular in nature, though they may have roots in Eastern traditions, and their purpose is to:

- Reduce stress, anxiety, and tension
- Minimize negative thoughts
- Raise levels of self-awareness
- Increase awareness of unconscious biases
- Develop positive perspectives
- Improve the ability to focus
- Boost productivity levels
- Improve relationships
- Develop personal positive traits

To some, these results might sound too good to be true. Therefore, please note that these outcomes arrive via a slow and gradual process. From our very childhood, we've been conditioned to think, behave, and respond to situations in certain ways, and transforming our behavior is no easy task. It's important to be clear about what we are hoping to gain from learning these techniques. If our aspiration is to simply reduce stress and anxiety so we can become more focused and productive, then it won't take too long. In fact, after I lead workshops, people feel better immediately during and after the session.

As we go deeper into the practice, we will be able to achieve higher levels of self-awareness, which will lead to greater opportunities for transformation and growth. We will discover aspects of ourselves that we hadn't previously seen. It can be a very eye-opening experience. There is absolutely no need, and it is futile, to compare our progress with another's because we have no idea of their particular conditioning and the amount of time they're dedicating to reflection and self-improvement. The best approach is to just focus on the process we have laid out for ourselves and pursue that on a consistent basis. I am 100% sure that we will be absolutely amazed at the transformation witnessed over the weeks, months, and years as we make these practices part of our regular life's routine. The results will not be the same for any two people, and our upbringing, cultural environment, parents, and friends play important roles in our progress.

**Deep dive into self-awareness**

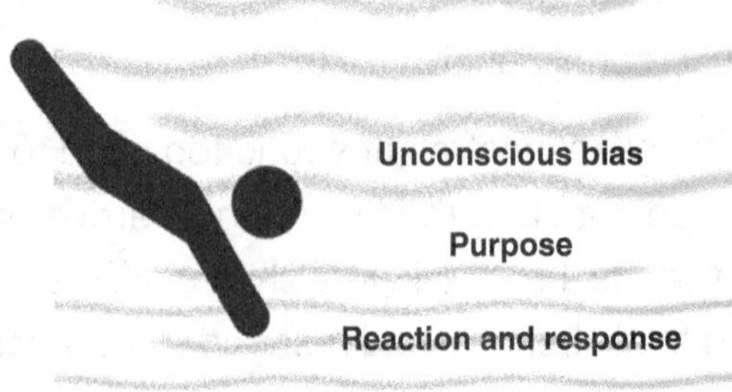

## Coming into the Present Moment

When we first sit down to meditate, there is a good chance that there are many plans, ideas, and thoughts rushing through our head. The last conversation, interaction, or email may still be sitting in the inbox of our mind. One technique I find helpful in getting the mind focused and present is to think about one specific thing. Generally, when I lead sessions at a company or conference, I'll have people close their eyes, sit comfortably, put their feet flat on the floor, and bring all of their attention to the weight of their feet pushing down into the floor, which helps to ground us. The challenge is to continue to focus on the weight of the feet. We have given the mind a very specific task to perform, which makes it easier to not get distracted. This exercise also serves as a challenge for individuals to try and stay focused on one thing. I tell the participants that if they begin planning or thinking about the past, which is bound to happen, they should recognize what they were thinking about and gently bring their awareness back to their feet. There's no need to get frustrated or upset if the mind wanders off, because that's just what the mind does.

**Single-pointed focus**

The next step it is to bring the attention to the weight of the body pushing down into their seat. It's a very simple exercise, but participants begin to realize how challenging it is to keep the mind focused on one thing. It's sort of like having a puppy on a leash – there is no way it's going to be able to walk in a straight line. A puppy will get distracted by every sight, sound, and smell, and our mind is not very different.

After spending about 10 seconds focusing on the feet, and another 10 seconds focusing on the weight of the body, I ask people to lean back into their chair, bringing the attention to the weight of the body pushing backward. Next, I ask individuals to bring awareness to their hands and fingers and how they are situated. Are their hands on the armrest of the chair or on their thighs? Are the fingers intertwined with each other? The point is just to become aware and keep everything relaxed.

Now, I ask if it is possible for their mind to focus on all of the above simultaneously. Can they become aware of their feet on the floor, the weight of their body pushing down in the seat, and the position of their back and fingers all at the same time? Try this for the next 15–20 seconds and see if it's possible. This is a fun and challenging exercise and most people come to realize that the mind can't focus on more than one or two things at a time. The more we do this, the more we realize that in reality, the mind actually only focuses on one thing before switching to the next. This connects back to the earlier point about multitasking and how it isn't really possible.

## Learning to Breathe

Now that the mind has come into the present moment and we have been able to go internal, we can go to the next phase: breathing. Breathing is something we do every single day. It's an involuntary act; no one taught us how to do it. Our first breath happened the moment we exited the womb and we've just kept on going without giving it much thought. It's time to become a little more intentional with our breath and experience the benefits of deep and focused breathing.

### Deep Breathing

Let's begin by making sure our eyes are closed and then taking a slow, deep breath, filling our lungs completely, visualizing their expansion and feeling the chest broaden.

Once the lungs are filled, slowly exhale, completely emptying out the lungs. Take another five to 10 breaths in the same way and try your best to stay focused on the breath going in and out of your lungs. This is not only helping us stay in the present moment, but it's allowing the lungs to take in slightly more breath each time. Moreover, the mind has something specific to focus on and some place to come to when it gets distracted or begins daydreaming during the session.

### Breathing Through the Nose

Next, try and breathe just through the nasal passages, keeping the mouth closed. If this is too challenging, perhaps because your nose is clogged, then feel free to use your mouth. I don't want anyone to feel suffocated because they're not able to breathe properly. If you're able to only breathe through the nose, feel the cool breath going in and filling your lungs completely and then breathe out the breath that has been warmed up by your body. As you're inhaling and exhaling, feel the cool breath entering your body and the warmer breath leaving your body. Continue for another five to 10 breaths.

### Diaphragmatic Breathing

We want not only our lungs to get involved in the breathing process, but also our belly. During inhalation, we should feel the belly rising and relaxing during the exhalation. This is described by Harvard Health as "diaphragmatic" or "abdominal breathing"[1] and that it can "slow the heartbeat and can lower

---

[1]"Learning Diaphragmatic Breathing," Harvard Health Publishing, March 10, 2016. https://www.health.harvard.edu/healthbeat/learning-diaphragmatic-breathing

or stabilize blood pressure." Who would have thought our breath could impact our health to such a degree?

### Holding the Breath

Now we're going to practice holding our breath for very short periods of time. When we hold our breath, the body will start to tense up a little bit. One of our goals is to take notice as we tense up and then relax ourselves while we are holding our breath. This is a great exercise that trains our mind to stay relaxed during times of conflict and disagreement. Generally, during stressful moments, our muscles in our face and body start tensing up. However, it's important to know that even in those moments we have the power to keep ourselves calm and relaxed. Once we learn to do this, we can approach each difficult situation with more ease and clarity.

Begin by taking a deep breath in, filling the lungs completely, and holding your breath for three seconds. While in the process of holding your breath, try and relax your face, neck, back, and the rest of your body and then exhale. Once you've exhaled completely, hold your breath again. You want to hold your breath while your lungs are empty, which may seem a little more difficult. Hold your breath for three seconds and then take another deep breath and hold it for four seconds – try your best to not tense up – and then exhale. Hold your breath for four seconds once you've completely exhaled and then take another breath and hold for five seconds and do the same after exhaling. If for any reason it's too difficult to hold your breath for more than one or two seconds, that's completely fine. The idea is to relax yourself and not tense up.

One interesting fact to note is that the mind doesn't wander off during the time we are holding our breath; it actually stays put. I'm not sure why this happens. Perhaps it's wondering when you're going to start breathing again. This provides an indication that there is an interesting connection between our mind and our breath.

**Observing the fishbowl of the mind**

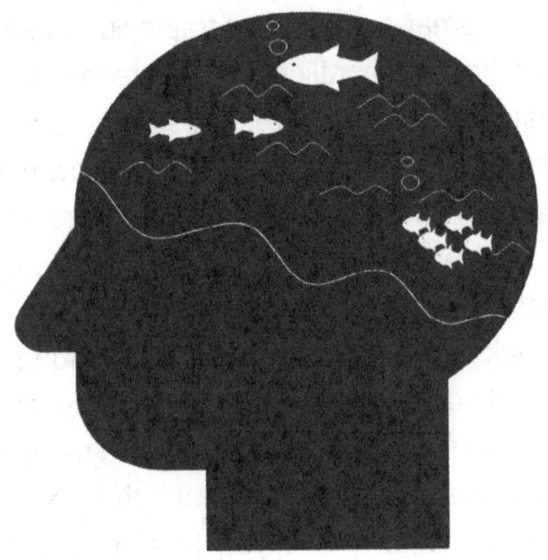

## Focusing and Awareness

Now that we have come into the present moment and relaxed our body and mind to some degree, let's bring our awareness to the very top of our head. First, we bring our awareness to our forehead, right between our eyebrows. From here, we want to become aware of the different thoughts, ideas, and plans swimming around in our head. As we confront these different thoughts, it is important not to engage with them, merely observe them as you would a fish in a fishbowl. We are taking inventory of our thinking to become aware of what's really on our mind. Do this for about 30 seconds. If you catch yourself diving into any particular idea, disconnect and continue to look at the broader picture of your thoughts.

### Letting Go of Thoughts

Take a deep breath in and as you exhale, let go of all the thoughts ideas and plans that you recognized earlier and allow your mind to completely empty out, even if it's just for a few seconds. Take another deep breath and this time as you exhale, breathe out any tension and stress that you're holding in your forehead and relax your forehead.

### Destressing the Eyes

Now we can bring awareness to our eyes. Take a deep breath in, then exhale out any tension you are holding in your eyes. The eyes become very stressed from looking at screens all day long. This is another exercise we can do throughout the day.

### Relaxing the Face

Taking another deep breath, filling your lungs completely, then exhale, breathing out any tension you're holding in the rest of your face, mouth, and jaw. Letting your mouth drop down and allowing the tongue to relax on the bottom of the mouth allows the face to experience total relaxation.

### Releasing the Neck and Shoulders

With the next inhalation, lift the shoulders up to your ears and hold them there for a count of three seconds. As you exhale, drop your shoulders, releasing the tension in your neck, shoulders, and upper back. Feel free to repeat this a couple of more times.

### Feeling the Heartbeat

We now want to bring our awareness into the region of the heart, and we do this by sitting very still and quietly, trying to pick up on the beating of the heart. This requires a tremendous amount of focus, especially if you are not used to having an awareness of your heartbeat. No need to worry if you aren't able to pick up on your heartbeat; I promise it's there. It takes time to learn to cut out the other noise in your head. Take another deep breath in and during the exhalation, breathe out any insecurities and fears that might be residing in the heart. By doing this, we can lighten the load of the heart. Sadness, loneliness, and depression are moods we all go through at different times in our life that weigh heavily on the heart. It's important to put some focus on the heart and try and release some of the heaviness once in a while.

## Discovering Gratitude

While we are in this heart space, let's take a moment to feel grateful for three things that are happening in our life. These could be things that are currently happening or experiences that have happened in the past. They don't have to be big things. I prefer that we remember all the little things that are happening. Too often we start thinking about things that didn't go right or opportunities we missed out on. We ask the age-old question "Why is this happening to me?" When our mind gets flooded with such thoughts, we need to be able to step on the brakes and stop these thoughts from bringing us down, to shift gears and start driving forward. At any given moment, there are so many positive things that are happening in our life and we just need to stop and observe them.

Once, when my business slowed down significantly, I began to worry about what could happen next. This is all I could think about. A few simple things occurred that helped me refocus and change my mindset. I remember I had gone to the grocery store to pick up a few items. When I got back and tried to put the food in the fridge, it would barely fit. There were so many things already in there that I was having a hard time adding more. In that moment, as I was staring at the full fridge, my heart began to fill with gratitude. I thought to myself that work may be a bit slow right now, but I won't be sleeping on an empty stomach. Having food to eat is no small thing. If we took inventory of the quantity of good food we throw away in America, it could probably bring an end to world hunger.

When my family first came to this country in 1980, I was only seven years old. My parents came with very little money and were working seven days a week, struggling to make enough to get by. My parents later told me that at one point they could barely afford to buy milk for me. Of course, I was too little to realize how bad things were. They never let me feel the struggles they were experiencing. However, I can understand why they never waste food. Unless something is absolutely horrible, we eat everything on our plate. They have taught me to respect food because not having it is a very humbling experience and can bring out the worst in humanity. Even when I eat out, I have a hard time leaving a little on the plate. The importance of not wasting food is deeply ingrained in me. Take as much as you can finish was and continues to be the message. My regular visits to India, where you can't avoid seeing starving people on the street begging for food, is not only heartbreaking, but reinforces the value of food, which we can so often take for granted.

That same week that I was worrying about my work, it was my birthday. I invited some of my closest friends to come over for lunch. We all sat around the dining table for hours talking, laughing, eating, reminiscing, and just having a great time. I remember thinking to myself that I was so fortunate and felt so grateful to have friends who I could relate to and who were there for me and that I had parents who care for me. I realized I was a very wealthy human being. Then I started noticing all the little things I had ignored that had added tremendous value to my life, and as this was happening, my eyes began to tear up with feelings of gratitude. Yes, money and a stable financial life are important, but I understood all of the little things that matter the most. In actuality, we are all wealthy in some way or another; we merely need to take time to recognize our wealth. As long as we look at the wealth of others, we will never truly appreciate the wealth we have been given in the form of family, friends, talents, food, and health. When we take this all into consideration, it shouldn't be difficult to discover three things to feel grateful for. When we do this consistently, we begin to discover more items in our life to be grateful for. When we're grateful, we feel happy. Without gratitude we can never really be completely happy.

With enough practice, gratitude can become a habit. Whenever I experience hardships or remember the adversities I have undergone, I try and reflect on how at any given moment, things could have gotten much worse. It's not that those moments won't sometimes shake us to the core, but developing a gratitude mindset will give us the strength to weather the storm and become fixed like a deep-rooted tree that may lose its leaves and flowers during a hurricane but will remain standing and begin the regeneration process. Developing the right mindset is the key to becoming resilient. Whenever I look back at some of the crazy experiences life threw at me, I realize that it wouldn't have taken much for the situation to go completely out of control and could have led to an even bigger financial, physical, or emotional disaster. I definitely wouldn't want any of those situations to repeat themselves. However, I feel grateful for having survived them and gaining wisdom and insight about life and its unpredictability.

If we don't learn to move through life with an attitude of gratitude, we run the risk of getting bitter and negative, living life with the "why me?" or "why not me?" approach. It's not always easy to feel grateful, especially when more things are going wrong than right. Usually, after a certain amount of time has passed, when we look back and have time to analyze what happened, it becomes more feasible for us to feel grateful. One would need to be at a very high level of consciousness to experience gratitude while in the midst of mayhem, and there are those who have achieved that state of being. However, it's not something we can artificially achieve. It starts with a daily practice of experiencing and feeling grateful for whatever is happening in our life, whether it's prosperity or a setback because all of it, especially the setbacks, help us grow and mature.

## Self-Development and Personal Growth

Meditation isn't just about sitting and focusing on the breath. It is supposed to help us improve our character and behavior. With enough introspection, it should allow us to increasingly feel gratitude in our life, and also enables us to raise our self-awareness and develop the positive qualities we need to become a better human being. In my humble opinion, if whatever meditation practice one is engaging in isn't making them a kinder, more empathetic, and thoughtful human being, then the meditation isn't really working on the deepest level.

The goal of this meditation is to focus on developing qualities that will make us a better human being. Begin by sitting comfortably and going through one or more of the breathing exercises described earlier. Focus on one quality that you would like to develop and improve upon. It's important to remember that the quality we want to focus on should be aimed at improving our character. Most likely, you'll be trying to decide which one to focus on because, in all honesty, we all need development on many levels. Each time we engage in this meditation, we can focus on a different quality. We can also focus on one for an entire week and then switch to another during the next week. Some obvious ones to consider are being less judgmental, forgiveness, and patience.

### Being Less Judgmental

I think our minds would be blown away if we understood how often and how quickly we judge others. We have programmed ourselves to form opinions about others, which usually aren't very accurate, especially if we're coming to a conclusion about someone on the street who we don't know or have never interacted with before. The moment we begin looking at someone for more than a couple of seconds, there is a good chance that we're sizing them up and deciding if they're good, bad, kind, cruel, cool, attractive, ugly, smart, stupid, fashionable, unfashionable, athletic, or out of shape. The list doesn't stop there but is a good indication of how the mind categorizes people and puts them in boxes. It's also completely possible that we are attracted to that person but simultaneously deciding if we could be with them. Creating an impression about someone based on their external look and behavior is fairly shallow and superficial. How many times has it happened that we formed an opinion of someone, and when we got to know them, we realized how off we were and how different that person was?

A fun activity we can try is to catch ourselves each time we are in the process of judging another person. Take note of whether the judgment was negative or positive. The results might surprise you. Many times, when we meet someone who might be better than us in some capacity, we begin to feel inferior. To counteract that feeling of inferiority, the mind then begins to find some fault with that individual just so we can feel good about ourselves. The truth is that there are probably several ways in which that person is better than us and there are many things that we are good at. Putting someone down is the ego's defense mechanism of falsely trying to make ourselves feel better.

Wouldn't it be great if we could retrain our mind to think positively about people instead of judging them? Just imagine what it would be like to walk down the street and every time the mind started to focus on someone, it imagined a positive quality about them. This mindset has the potential to transform so many of our personal and professional relationships. Instead of judging a certain family member, friend, or colleague we don't see eye-to-eye with, we endeavor to see their positive side. Of course, this doesn't mean we give up discriminating between right and wrong, or ethical and unethical actions. What this means is that we don't jump to conclusions and immediately begin to assassinate someone's character before getting to know them. We all have the right to feel upset, sad, and frustrated when things aren't going right, but hopefully we don't get permanently labeled by each other because of one moment of weakness. If we don't want these labels, then we need to be able to offer that courtesy to others.

### Comparisons

Not only does judging others create negativity in our mind, which is terrible for our health, but when we begin comparing ourselves to others, it can lead us into depression and frustration. Looking at someone else's success, wealth, and fame can bring us down, especially if we were hoping to attain the same level of accomplishment. No matter how much we have, there will always be others who have more money, influence, power, a better-looking spouse, higher-achieving kids, fancier cars, and more beautiful homes. This naturally leads to feelings of envy toward those we are comparing ourselves to. When envy gets bad enough, we might even start to wish some misfortune to befall others. Envying others seems to be part of human nature, but that doesn't make it okay. The more competitive an individual is in their pursuits, the greater the chances they will be bothered by the success of another. Of course, if we have a competitive nature, then we have a competitive nature. There's no way and no need to turn that down, and there's nothing wrong with it. The drive to compete can be transformed to stay focused on one's own goals and accomplishments. We can allow others' successes to inspire and motivate us to do better but there doesn't need to be the feeling that "I need to outdo someone else" to feel good about ourselves. The best approach is to set a goal, surpass it, and then set another one. There is nothing wrong with ambition and a desire to succeed. Ambition means we're alive and is a sign that we have something to strive for. Without ambition, we run the risk of becoming couch potatoes without a real purpose in life. We just want to be able to maintain a healthy ambition, which is one that doesn't involve negativity toward the accomplishment of others.

Just as everything in life has a positive side and a negative side, the same is true for the presence of social media. We're able to get more news from more sources at a much faster rate than ever before, which makes it so easy to stay in touch with friends and family who may be in different parts of the world. It also creates an environment where we can easily scroll through profiles and wish we could have the experiences others are having. Everyone loves posting pictures of their travel, the things they're buying, and all the cool things they're doing. It would be a nice exercise to examine our motivation for posting. Is it to show off and make others envious of the good things we're experiencing? Sometimes, we see others envying us as a sign of success. However, why are we letting that be a measure of our happiness? Should our goal be to serve others and to feel happy with who we've become, rather than achieve so much that it starts to bother others? To reiterate my point, it's perfectly fine to gain all the prosperity you want, but the intention behind it shouldn't be fueled by the desire of wanting to feel better than others.

## Forgiveness

This is a very important quality to include as part of our regular meditation routine. Part of the goal behind meditation is to develop a peaceful mindset. We're not going to be able to achieve that peace unless we are trying to forgive those who have hurt us. Whether it's a good friend who let us down, a family member who wasn't there for us, or a colleague we felt backstabbed by, holding on to grudges and resentment is not a peaceful state of existence. It's like a heavy burden that we're carrying around wherever we go. These burdens go with us to work or when we go on vacation. Forgiveness is something human beings struggle with. How much we are able to forgive someone depends on the severity of what they did or didn't do.

It can take years or even decades for some wounds to heal, and even then they can leave a scar. In general, human beings struggle with the idea of forgiving, and no doubt, it's not something that is easily achieved. It's in our own best interest to try and forgive, because the weight of the memories is resting on our heart and, over time, the heaviness of past experiences can prevent us from being peaceful.

### Patience

I think we're all running on empty when it comes to patience. How much could our relationships progress if we could simply be a little more patient with our family members, colleagues, and even strangers? Have you had the experience of being in your car at an intersection and the light turns green? You haven't even had the chance to take your foot off the brake to press the gas pedal when the person behind you honks because you took one second to step on the gas. It totally makes you want to pull out your hair. In all fairness, perhaps we've done that to others. I know in my younger days, I needed to be the first one to cross the intersection as if the guy next to me was trying to race me. Even though I didn't honk at people, I had very little patience. Perhaps now my karma is catching up to me.

In my opinion, the more our conveniences increase, the more impatient we become. Everything is at our fingertips and we need things done as easily and quickly as possible. We can buy a house, a car, make flight and hotel reservations, and even find a life partner with a few taps on our smart device. Because we love our conveniences and get used to them, the moment an app malfunctions or a web browser takes too long, we can get frustrated and even angry. The worst part is that our impatient behavior can spill over into our professional and personal relationships. We might become very demanding with our colleagues and have unreasonable expectations, which can create a dent in our relationships. Not only is there a high probability of an employee walking out, but it also creates a toxic environment in the workplace, where employees begin to feel uncertain about their future. When this tendency and approach enter our family life, it can create all kinds of tensions. Strained relationships will affect our workplace performance and vice versa. It's essential that we learn to be patient, especially with our family members, even though they are the hardest ones to be patient with. We must learn to accept others for who they are and not try to get them to change the way we want them to be.

My time at the monastery, where I was living with so many different personalities, taught me to see the special talents each individual had. Each monk had a variety of skills, and too often I wanted them to be able to do things the way I did them. When they couldn't, I would get frustrated. Gradually, I began to realize that many of them were far more capable at other tasks than I was. It's important to understand that if we want others to be patient with us, then we need to extend them the same courtesy.

### Compassion

When meditating on becoming more compassionate, we can reflect on how we can develop compassion in our day-to-day life. First of all, we have to want to develop compassion, recognize times in our life where we fell short in this department, not make excuses for our lack of it, and simply own it. Then and only then can the transformation begin. It's quite unpleasant to recognize and remember the moments when we were callous instead of compassionate, but that honest acceptance is a sign of humility. Did we ignore someone in our family, friend circle, or workplace who needed our help, because we were too busy to reach out to them? In retrospect, if we take time to contemplate those moments, we can probably admit that in most such cases, we could have helped them out without it having a significant impact on our work and life. Was it that we didn't actually have time to express compassion, that we didn't care, or was it that we were lazy? I am the first to admit that I have recognized all of the above within my own self and feel ashamed that I convinced myself that what I was doing was more important, and that I didn't have time to help someone out. Remembering those moments helps me as I move forward in my own development. The more we are able to stop and offer assistance to those who need it, the easier it will be to do it in the future. We will realize that helping others doesn't always take as much time and energy as we thought it would. Small gestures of service can actually be big and incredibly meaningful to those in need.

Two amazing things happen when we are able to take the time to stop and demonstrate compassion. The first is that it feels great and we become happy. From what I studied during my time as a monk, the desire to serve others is inherently built into the core of our being. When we deny this feeling, it gets pushed back, leading to selfish behavior. Every time we stop and extend a helping hand, we feel joy because we brought joy into someone else's life. Seeing their gratitude and happiness makes us happy. So, as we try all kinds of complicated ways to find happiness, it actually lies in the simple, yet what we perceive as difficult, act of service.

### Selflessness

The other interesting, yet more difficult, concept that I studied in the monastery was that selfless service to others is vital to our growth. When I first learned about this new facet to service, I loved it. Then I quickly began to realize that it's rather difficult. No doubt, there are many occasions where we offer a helping hand just because someone needed it and didn't expect anything in return. At other times, we offer our assistance with the hope of getting something in return. Sometimes, we might even make it clear that we're going to help someone out because we expect something in return. The more we get into the mood of exchanging favors for favors, the less we value the importance of selfless service. After all, it is our time that we're giving to another person and nothing is more valuable than the short amount of time we have been given. How we spend that time is important, and we do need to evaluate if the service we are offering to others is doing some good. For example, if I decide to give someone money and they use that money to get inebriated, then I wouldn't consider that act of service to be useful.

As a monk, I never received compensation for any of the work that I did. This work consisted of lecturing, personal coaching, cooking, serving food, or just lending an ear to someone struggling. If anyone did offer a donation, I would give it to the monastery, which was providing for all of my personal maintenance needs. Serving without motivation was an amazing experience, and it allowed me to develop many wonderful friendships. Sometimes, when I look back at those 15 years, from ages 27 to 42, I reflect on the idea that if I hadn't lived as a monk, I could have developed a very successful personal career and financial stability. Then I realize I'm not sure what kind of human being I would be if I had a ton of money and wasn't trained in the principles of service, humility, and compassion. I realize that whatever we give to others out of compassion all comes back to us in some shape of form. While in the monastery, I never would have imagined myself traveling around the country and speaking to high-level executives at Fortune 500 companies, just like I didn't plan to become a monk. I truly feel that the service I did while I was a monk is now being reciprocated with. We're not missing out on anything while serving others, we are only gaining. We should be eager when the precious opportunities to serve others arise. We need to see these moments of serving and bringing joy to another as a gift life is providing us.

## Bringing It All Together

A steady and consistent practice of mindfulness will help us develop the humility to recognize our shortcomings and weaknesses. We probably already have an idea of what they are but might not have fully acknowledged them. We have spent hundreds of hours in front of the mirror looking to make sure everything on the outside looks good and checks out. Now we are beginning the process of looking inside, perhaps for the first time, and there's a whole universe in there that is yet unexplored. There are many beautiful aspects of ourselves that are waiting to be discovered and simultaneously, there are some rough, not so pleasant, and darker aspects of our personality that will be revealed. This is where we will need to be able to put aside our ego and be able to truly look at ourselves and acknowledge the different components to our personality that we have developed through our various life experiences.

The ego makes us believe that there's nothing to fix or improve upon. It convinces us that we are fine just the way we are. It prevents us from being able to take an honest look at one's self. It was quite a humbling experience when, about 25 years ago, after some months of meditating regularly, I started to notice some of my darker spots. Initially, I wanted to reject the idea that I had things to improve upon but over time, I began to accept that I needed to make some changes. I can say that a quarter-century later, I am still a work in progress, and I hope to continue to have the strength to keep on learning and changing. Many times, you can feel like giving up and feel like more progress isn't possible or is too difficult. However, I personally don't want to be the same exact person 10 years from now. I want to have grown and developed into a more mature and thoughtful person, and this can only happen if I am determined to move forward.

I have found that the meditation process not only gives us the self-awareness of the changes we need to make but also provides us the strength to continue the process and keep making progress. It can be challenging to remain determined if we're doing it alone and therefore, it is very important to find others who are on this path of growth, self-development, and mindfulness. I've heard some monks give the example of how a single twig can be snapped in two very easily, but if you have a stack of twigs, it becomes almost impossible to break them. Therefore, we need to be able to connect with others, whether it's at work or in our personal life, who are on the same path and be able to share our experiences with each other. This isn't true just for mindfulness, it's true for practically every type of activity. There are tens of thousands of associations where people with a similar occupation or interest come together to learn from and inspire each other. Why not use the same approach for our own personal practice? Doing it alone isn't impossible; it's a whole lot easier when we surround ourselves with others who are moving through the same challenges and fighting the good fight.

Meditation can be perceived as a solo endeavor and ultimately our practice is going to be very individual and some components might be unique. Once in a while, it's helpful to be able to discuss our challenges and progress with others who are in the same boat. In the monastery, we would all meditate together at 5:00 a.m. When my mind began to wander off, I found it easier to bring it back when I was surrounded by others who were trying to do the same thing. When I compare the quality of my meditation from when I was living in the monastery to living at home, I do notice a significant difference in terms of quality. Being in the company of other serious practitioners helped me stay focused for longer periods of time. Now that I meditate alone, I find that my mind wanders off more quickly and for longer periods of time. Yes, even though I spent 15 years as a monk, my mind still wanders. It hasn't yet become still like the flame of a candle in a windless place.

As one fifteenth-century monk, Rupa Goswami, said, "when one starts their inward journey, one needs to be enthusiastic, confident and patient." Enthusiasm is needed for any endeavor to be successful. Many moments will come that will test our resolve, but we need to keep pushing forward. Our mind, while on the path of rehabilitation, will resist and rebel and tell us that we're wasting our time and we could be using our efforts for other valuable purposes. The mind has become set in its ways and doesn't want change. Therefore, to be able to overcome the rants of the mind, we need to be able to remember the positive experiences we have had during our meditation practices and develop the confidence of knowing that it will only get better. Even within a few weeks, we should be able to notice some changes in our attitude and thought process. Most likely, those we interact with closely will also start to pick up on a shift in our approach and behavior, which should serve as fuel to keep going forward. The only reason we should look back is to see how far we have come from where we were.

Patience is going to be key because there will be many dry patches when we just don't feel like we're progressing. There will be times when we feel like we're still in the same exact place even though we've been gradually increasing our practice. It will be natural to feel discouraged when this happens. However, it's important to understand that progress isn't always perceivable. Growth isn't always visible to us, but it is happening as long as we are following the process in a healthy and positive manner. This means that we're remaining steady with the practice, while trying to improve our character and coming together with others who have similar aspirations. When a seed is burrowed into the ground, it will not sprout immediately. It requires watering and care. For some plants, the growth can be slow, but it is happening. This is where patience will come in handy. We need to trust the process.

## Summary

- Deep breathing is a key component of the mindfulness practice. Simply remembering to take a few deep breaths throughout the day can help us stay calm and maintain a proper perspective on our current situation.

- During the day, become aware of the tension points in your body and try and relax those areas. We don't need to wait till the weekend to destress; we can do it throughout the day.
- Shifting to a positive mindset can be achieved with the simple practice of gratitude. Feeling grateful for the basic things in life, such as food, clothing, shelter, friends, and family can uplift us whenever we're feeling we didn't get something we deserved or worked hard for.
- No great achievement in life just happens. It requires concerted planning and effort. Becoming a kinder, more thoughtful, and compassionate human won't happen automatically. We need to have a desire to grow and develop and then actively meditate on endeavoring to make such changes.
- Meditation will help us develop the humility we need, to recognize our weaknesses and shortcomings. It will tame the ego that is telling us that there is nothing that needs to change and that we are fine the way we are.

## Reflection Questions and Exercises

Before you begin your practice, prepare your environment:

1. Put away your phone or put it on sleep mode for the duration of your practice. If you know you only have a certain amount of time for the practice, you can use the countdown timer on your phone.
2. Become aware of how you are feeling (tense, anxious, sad, happy, etc.) before you begin.

3. Start with some of the breathing exercises described previously.
4. What are the three things you are grateful for? Each day, you can try to find one or two different things you are grateful for. Use the following table to get started.

| | Gratitude |
|---|---|
| **Monday** | |
| **Tuesday** | |
| **Wednesday** | |
| **Thursday** | |
| **Friday** | |
| **Saturday** | |
| **Sunday** | |

5. Six qualities were listed in this chapter. To get started, write down how you plan to further develop these qualities within your character. Additional space has been provided so you can add other areas you would like to focus on.

| Quality | What steps will you take to develop these qualities? |
|---|---|
| Being less judgmental | |
| Comparing yourself to others | |
| Forgiveness | |
| Patience | |
| Compassion | |
| Selflessness | |

6. At the end of your practice, reflect on and write down how the meditation has impacted your mood and stress levels. Comparing your frame of mind before the session and after will help you understand how it is influencing your mindset and behavior.

# Afterword

In July 2013, I finished my first book, *Urban Monk: Exploring Karma, Consciousness, and the Divine*, which was my attempt to answer a question people frequently asked me: "What made you want to become a monk?"

A lot has changed since then, with the most significant difference being that I'm no longer a monk and no longer live on the Lower East Side of New York, where I spent almost 15 years in the monastic order. People are now asking me, "What made you stop wanting to be a monk?"

I suppose I have some kind of karma where I must keep talking about my passage in and out of the monastic life, so here I am writing my second book to shed some light on this latest journey.

## On the Move

Transitioning out of monastic living was not easy by any stretch of the imagination. I joined the monastery in 1999 when I was 27 years old, thrust into the life of a monk after experiencing several major upheavals throughout my lifetime. It was during my thirteenth year in the monastery, while I was writing *Urban Monk*, that I began to consider the idea of leaving the monastery behind and pursuing family life instead. Many of the monks I had developed close friendships with had decided to pursue other dreams such as going back to school for graduate degrees, developing professional careers, or sharing their life in a loving marriage. As I watched more of my companions leave the monastery, my resolve to remain a monk began to weaken, and my desires for a family and career grew stronger.

What was I going to do? How would I earn a living? How would I go about finding a life partner? These were the questions that began to occupy my mind. I was 40 years old and had spent a good chunk of my young adulthood in a monastery. I had only a couple of years of college and work experience under my belt. I knew this shift was going to be uncomfortable, and I would have to navigate plenty of unknown territories. This transition would be the most powerful change in my life.

I'm no stranger to change. The first major transition I experienced was my parents' emigration from India to the United States in 1980. I was seven years old, their only child, and I barely spoke English. This meant that while my parents were working seven days a week, selling gift items at Venice Beach, I was left to navigate a very foreign culture and figure out my identity all on my own. We came to this country with little to no money. My parents had an incredible work ethic and were putting in 12-hour days. Each day involved packing up our 1972 Toyota station wagon and driving 30 minutes to Venice Beach, setting up our shop, sitting under the hot sun, selling a variety of gift items all day long, and then returning home. Taking a day off just wasn't an option because we were living day to day. There came a time when my parents didn't have enough money to even buy milk for me. I was very young and didn't realize what they were going through and they made sure I wasn't aware of the daily hardships they were undergoing. They did an amazing job at sheltering me from the challenges they were facing on a daily basis so I never really felt the struggles they were dealing with.

Within about eight years, my parents' dedication, incredible work ethic, and hard work allowed them to establish a multimillion-dollar jewelry business, which led us to lead a very lavish lifestyle in Glendale, California. From my bedroom window in our three-story, six-bedroom, five-bathroom house on the hill, with a swimming pool, Jacuzzi and waterfall, I had a postcard view of downtown Los Angeles and beyond. In fact, between our isolation as the last property on the hill and our incredible scenic opportunity, we had baby snakes, deer drinking water from our pool, and local teenagers driving up on the weekends to look at the view. Most immigrants who enter this country come to chase the American dream and we began living it a lot faster than we had expected. The relentless hard work was definitely a tremendous factor in the success my parents achieved, but other unknown and unexplainable factors such as luck, destiny, and karma can't be ruled out as additional factors to that prosperity. After all, many people labor day and night but don't get the breaks that are often needed to thrive the way they would like to. It is easy to take all the credit for our achievements; however, it is important to remain humble throughout and recognize that some or many factors in our success were beyond our control.

## The Fire

The second major transition came in 1992 when our jewelry factory caught on fire, causing us to lose most of our inventory and clients. This tragedy forced us to file bankruptcy and close everything down. We lost not only the business but also the house, other properties, and vehicles. I had to drastically cut back on day-to-day spending and began minimizing going out with my friends. In fact, I began to distance myself from my social community because I had just gone from being the wealthiest kid in my class who was always inviting friends over for gatherings and pool parties to spending more time by myself. The first reason was that I had to all of a sudden be careful about the money that I was spending and secondly, I felt embarrassed to let my friends know that we were undergoing financial struggles. I was identifying my self-worth by the possessions I had and was afraid that my position in my social circle would diminish if I wasn't able to maintain the lifestyle that I had earlier.

Before the fire, I never worried about money and never had to work for it. Being an only child, I was used to getting everything I wanted and hadn't fully appreciated the efforts my parents had put forth to support our lifestyle. After the fire, my appreciation for money and its value developed in a way it never had before.

During this time, I didn't know how to communicate to my friends what was transpiring within our lives. I was ashamed to admit that our life was completely falling apart and that we were about to lose everything. I didn't know how to deal with the immense loss we were experiencing, and never told any of my friends that we were about to leave Los Angeles for good. It was as if I had fallen off the face of the earth, and many of my friends never knew what happened to me until I showed up to my 20-year high school reunion with a shaved head and wearing the robes of a monk!

## Post-Communist Bulgaria

This devastating loss led to my third major transition, where, after losing everything, my dad decided to explore new business opportunities in post-communist Bulgaria. Under this topsy-turvy regime, we spent two years in an unpredictable and sometimes unsafe environment. Those were probably the most confusing and soul-searching times I had ever experienced. I felt like the rug had been pulled out from under me, and I was asking myself how and why this was happening, and what had I done to deserve it? In 1993, when I arrived in Bulgaria, hardly anyone there spoke English. The languages spoken by the locals were Bulgarian and Russian. I couldn't understand any of the television programming because none of it was in English. All the American movies in the theaters were several years old and I had seen them all. All the apartment buildings looked the same. I went from living in a mansion-like property in Los Angeles to a one-bedroom apartment that was smaller than my parents' master bedroom had been. Growing up in Southern California, swimming in the ocean, and playing basketball, tennis, and volleyball were the recreational activities I would engage in on an almost daily basis. However, none of this was available in the small town of Plovdiv, where we had relocated to in hopes of embarking on a new business venture. In essence, all of my hobbies came to a screeching halt and I felt like I had entered an episode of the *Twilight Zone*. My world had basically turned upside down and my social life came to a complete halt.

There was also no Internet with which I could distract myself and find an escape. Not being able to speak the language, communicate with anyone, or find any recreational outlet, I was left to ponder life and its meaning in a way I never had before. Having no more external distraction left, I began, in a serious manner, for the very first time, an inward journey that would become my saving grace and would help me navigate the day-to-day uncertainty of my time in Bulgaria. Most people begin their meditation practice at a yoga class or retreat or while visiting a monastery in the East; however, even though I had been meditating on and off while in Los Angeles, my serious practice of meditation began during the uprooting experience I was going through in Bulgaria. Additionally, I began studying a wisdom text from India known as the *Bhagavad Gita*. This was the perfect text for me because it talks about a family of five brothers, all of whom are warriors, who were cheated out of their kingdom and exiled to live in the forest for 13 years. I had never before been able to relate to this ancient text of spiritual wisdom, but now I was in a very different frame of mind and my life circumstances had shifted so dramatically that I was eagerly and desperately looking for some guidance and direction. I had heard many monks explain that the earthquakes and hurricanes of life are very helpful because they break us out of our comfort zone and humble us to the realities of life. It is usually only during these moments that one starts to seriously inquire about the goal of human life, which is usually very different than what we imagine it to be.

## Return to the United States

After two incredibly challenging years, my parents decided to relocate to New Jersey so we could be close to New York City. It is this move that led to my fourth significant transition, which was unique and special because I voluntarily initiated it.

All of my previous upheavals had taken place as a result of my parents' (mostly my dad's) decisions, and by this time I had become quite frustrated with the ups and downs I had experienced between 1992 and 1999. We had lost so much and moved around so frequently that I now felt a strong urge to get away from everything and take time to figure out my identity and decide how I wanted to live my life. It was probably the biggest decision I had made on my own thus far.

During my time in New Jersey, I had come in contact with some monks living in New York City, and they suggested that I go on a meditation retreat to India to live a life of simplicity and service. They explained to me that such an experience would help provide the clarity of purpose I was looking for, and they recommended a monastery in the bustling city of Mumbai, then known as Bombay. This congested, polluted, and highly populated city of 22 million people hardly seemed like the place to achieve clarity and inner peace. However, trusting their judgment, I quit my job as a loan officer at a mortgage company, packed my suitcase, and flew off to Mumbai in September 1999.

## Living with Monks in India

I had reasoned that a one-month retreat would provide enough time to achieve the growth and enlightenment I had set out to gain. Additionally, I wasn't too sure how long I would be able to survive the simple accommodations and rigors of monastic life. The monks slept on hardwood floors with only a straw mat, a blanket, and a mosquito net. They each had a closet measuring three feet wide, three feet high, and about a foot and a half deep. Due to limited space, I wasn't given a closet, so I was living out of my suitcase and sharing a tiny room with three other visitors from different parts of the world.

Our days began at 4 a.m., followed by meditation practices, studying, and listening to lectures from 5 to 9 a.m. This was the schedule every day, seven days a week, and with nothing distinguishing one day from another, I began losing track of time. There were no televisions in the monastery and hardly a facility to get online. Everything was communal: the sleeping area, the bathrooms, and the eating area. I had never lived in such an austere environment with so many rules and regulations.

My days were spent studying, helping in the kitchen, cleaning a part of the monastery, or spending time with the monks, getting to know them better. In the evenings, I would accompany some of the more senior monks to universities or other gatherings around the city, where they would give lectures. To my surprise, living out of a suitcase with minimal possessions, engaging in simple services, and traveling with the monks to their lectures really began to grow on me. It was an existence of selflessness and of helping others decipher the meaning and purpose of life.

When I was younger and living in Los Angeles, making a lot of money and driving fancy cars had been my life's goals. I had always been helpful to my friends, but the thought of living for others and working to enlighten society had never crossed my mind. A big aha moment was taking place for me, and a whole new paradigm of life was being revealed. My one-month retreat turned into six months of traveling to different monasteries and meditation centers, and the 4 a.m. wake-up call and two-hour meditation became my standard routine.

## Taking the Vow

Eventually, my six-month visa for India expired so I returned to New York City and moved in with the monks who had suggested that I train in India. I still hadn't committed to monastic life; I simply wanted to continue the beautiful and soul-nourishing existence I had experienced during my retreat. After two years of going back and forth about whether I could live this life permanently, I decided to make a short-term commitment and became a monk-in-training. As a student, I didn't make any formal vows, which left the door open in case I wanted to re-enter the working world and have a family. However, this commitment didn't turn out to be so short. I stayed for 15 years.

Living in a monastic setting in New York City was very different in almost every way from the experience in Mumbai. The common experience was the morning ritual of waking up very early in the morning, showering, and beginning the meditation practice. The big difference was that I was now living with about 10 other monks, most in their mid- to late twenties, some in their early thirties, and the head monk, who was of German origin, was in his early forties. The others were from different parts of the United States, and we even had a couple who were originally from Switzerland. Many monasteries are seen as training grounds, a sort of college or university, where one can come, study, meditate, develop one's personal character, learn to live a simple and humble life, and then take these teachings into the world as one begins their family life and pursues a vocation. In this way, during my 15 years, I must have seen over 50 individuals come, stay for a while, and then move on. How long each individual stayed was completely dependent on them and their own inspiration. Some stayed for a few months and some for many years. On occasion, if we felt an individual wasn't suited for the lifestyle, a polite suggestion would be made for him to pursue life in the regular world and continue to serve while living outside. This determination would be made if the person wasn't able to live in a communal setting where everything is shared or if it was challenging for them to get along with so many varying personalities.

The setting and environment of the monastery in New York was also quite different from the one in Mumbai. It was located on the Lower East Side and was surrounded by bars, restaurants, pizza places, and even a tattoo shop, which was immediately next to our entrance. We were situated on First Avenue, which meant that we were exposed to nonstop traffic and since there were two hospitals, also located on First Avenue, just 15 to 20 blocks away, we were constantly bombarded with the sound of ambulance sirens at all hours of the day and night. Our meditation room was situated on the third floor of the building and it faced First Avenue. The most interesting times of the week were Saturday and Sunday mornings. Our meditation practices would start around 4:30 a.m., and it was around that time that the bars would close. Once these establishments closed, the gatherings and drunken conversations would move out on to the sidewalk, which meant that while we had our eyes closed in meditation, we were able to hear the discussions that were taking place. Oftentimes, arguments and fights would break out and we could hear beer bottles breaking against the sidewalk. We would naturally begin to wonder how serious things were getting outside and if anyone had gotten hurt. Fortunately, there was a police precinct four blocks away and it wasn't long before the flashing blue and red lights of the police could be seen. One distinct memory I can't let go of is seeing two guys, without their shirts on, facing off in the middle of the street ready for a fistfight while cars were going around them.

New York City may not be the ideal place to practice serenity; however, it provides a very vivid and graphic scene of what can happen to our mind and consciousness if we don't take care of ourselves and learn to go inward.

It wasn't the meditation alone that inspired me to stay as a monastic for 15 years. I began to discover who I was, what my purpose was, and what brought me real happiness. During my second year, I was invited by an acquaintance, who was studying at Columbia University, to come and share some of the teachings I had been learning with the student community. I was excited about the possibility of sharing the amazing wisdom I had access to but simultaneously nervous because I was terrified of public speaking, even if it was to an audience of two to three individuals. This is quite ironic because speaking to corporate audiences is what I do now professionally. Most people have a hard time believing that I had a fear of public speaking. Getting up in front of people was something I had very successfully avoided for most of my life, but little did I know that I would have to confront this fear while living in a monastery. The first couple of years of doing presentations was quite challenging. However, the monastic tradition that I had joined strongly encouraged serving society by sharing what we ourselves were learning and practicing. Moreover, when students and corporate professionals would approach me and share with me how much the talk helped them, that would provide me with the encouragement and impetus to keep going. This was the first time in my life that I was making a small difference in people's lives, and I had never experienced such satisfaction from any other work.

## Why I Left the Monastery

If I was feeling such contentment in monastic life, why did I want to leave? When I turned 40 and watched several of the monks I had become friends with move on to pursue a life outside the monastery, I began to ponder my own future as a monastic. I also realized I thrived in a social setting with good friendships, and I didn't enjoy extended periods of solitude. Perhaps this is why I didn't feel overwhelmed by the hustle and bustle of New York City.

## Urban Dweller

As I thought about my comfort with urban living, it dawned on me that I had always been in one busy city after another. I was born in Kanpur, India, where the roads were continuously filled with massive varieties of two-wheeled, three-wheeled, four-wheeled, and eight-wheeled vehicles, constantly blasting their horns. Also sharing the streets were pedestrians, dogs, cows, and even some monkeys, which mainly stayed on the rooftops.

At the age of five, we moved to India's capital, Delhi, which was also a city filled with commotion. These first seven years of my life undoubtedly helped me develop a tolerance to traffic and congestion. The monastery in New York City was situated in one of the busiest parts of the city. Good earplugs become a monk's best friend and I had successfully learned to tune these sounds out.

## Becoming a Motivational Speaker

In spite of being in this busy and crowded city, as my friends departed the monastery, I began to feel lonely. Just as it had taken me years to resolve to live the life of a monk, it took years to get comfortable with the idea of transitioning out of monastic life. Neither was an overnight decision.

During my time in the monastery, I had lectured extensively at colleges, high schools, monasteries, and yoga studios, so I figured a career in motivational speaking could be a natural fit for me. In 2013, the year before I would move out of the monastery, I received several invitations to speak at Fortune

100 companies. The topics of my speeches were similar to the ones I currently focus on: Mindful Leadership, Workplace Culture and Mindfulness for Stress Management, and Work–Life Balance.

The first invitation came from an acquaintance who had heard me speak on multiple occasions and happened to work at one of the most prominent financial institutions in the country. I was asked if I would be willing to do the keynote speech for the company's annual global conference of approximately 1,500 attendees. I had never spoken to a corporate audience, let alone one of this size, but by now, I felt comfortable and confident being in front of any group. I accepted the invitation and was excited about this new challenge. When I was introduced to the meeting planner who was coordinating the entire event, she loved the idea of introducing mindfulness to financial professionals and of beginning the conference on such a unique note.

Although the meeting planner had initially agreed that I could speak in my monk robes, after further contemplation, she politely asked if I wouldn't mind dressing in business casual clothing. I had presented this option to her during our initial conversation, as showing up in my monk's robes at a conference for financial professionals might have been rather shocking. I can't remember whether I purchased my first pair of pants and a shirt in almost 15 years or dug them up from my closet at home. I believe I purchased the shirt, but the pants were a decade and a half old, and fortunately, they still fit.

Even though I had delivered over a thousand talks thus far, I was a bit nervous about speaking to a group of highly accomplished working professionals. I began my 60-minute talk by telling them how I had become a monk and concluded with some short mindfulness practices they could use at work.

After the speech, a lady approached me and very frankly told me that when she had first seen the agenda and noticed that a monk had been invited to speak, she was a little upset. She had wondered why the committee was inviting monks into their conferences, but then said, "now that I've heard your messages, I'm so glad I came." I received a lot of positive comments and feedback from that audience and left feeling absolutely thrilled about the whole experience. Thus began my journey into the world of corporate speaking.

Leaving monastic life had been on my mind for over a year, and I had discussed this lifestyle change with others in the community. Some of the monks were aware I was going down a new road, but no one, including myself, knew when and how this would take place. That November, I learned that my teacher, who had been a monk for over 40 years, was going to be visiting New York City from India. He had always been incredibly supportive of me while I was a monk, and when I first decided to commit to the monastic life, I remember him telling me that I was always free to change my mind and could leave monastic life and that there would be no shame in it. In fact, during the past couple of years of my monastic experience, he had suggested that I could shift into the regular world, but I tend to move slowly when it comes to life-changing decisions. I guess he understood what was going on in my heart and mind, so I reached out to him, asking if he could be present at my graduation ceremony, to which he happily agreed.

## Graduation Day

As a monk, I wore saffron-colored robes. When a monk graduates, he puts on white robes that let everyone know he is no longer a practicing monastic and is now an eligible bachelor. In December 2014, I sent an email to the community informing them that I would be transitioning out of monastic life later that month. The subject line of the email was "A White Christmas," and the first line of the letter said, "whether or not it snows on Christmas, I will be having a white Christmas." I went on to explain that I was moving on from monkhood and giving up my saffron robes, which would signify that I was no longer a monk and could now wear regular clothes.

Facing everyone in white cloth for the first time was a little embarrassing. There has long been a stigma against monks changing from saffron to white. A monastery is a place where people come and stay, for as long they are inspired. It can be seen as kind of a college or training ground where one can learn to abide by specific disciplines. Even though the books of wisdom explain that joining a monastery is a temporary phase in an individual's life, people are always surprised when a monk transitions out of monastic life and engages in material pursuits such as a career or marriage. I can't put my finger on it, but it is as if people want to see monks remain as monks for the rest of their lives. Perhaps, deep down, people are living vicariously through the strict and disciplined life of a monk, admiring a lifestyle they cannot achieve due to the demands of domestic life. This reverence puts pressure on the monastics to continue their life as a monk so as not to let people down. Somehow, monks are depicted as having transcended all emotions and human needs, and that's tough to live up to. This inaccurate perception creates a feeling of failure, as opposed to a sense of achievement and growth from a wonderful and positive experience. It is good to note that this attitude is changing in the West but has been slower to shift in the East.

None of these changes have been easy, but then again, I don't think they are meant to be. If change was simple, we would miss out on all the wisdom and growth it offers. Perhaps my transitions have been more drastic than most people's, but looking back, I can see how each of them has shaped and matured me in ways I couldn't possibly have planned. Steve Jobs once said, "you can only connect the dots looking back, you can't connect them looking forward."

There are some transitions, like going to college or relocating, that we know are coming, and we can plan ahead for them. It's the unexpected changes that are the most challenging because they force us to give up control, and this is very hard to do. Such upheavals humble us and help us realize we don't have the power we believe we do. The belief that we are in command provides us with false security and self-confidence, and when things begin to shift suddenly, we realize there is nothing we can do except let it happen. It is at this point where we start to develop humility and understand that life is not under our control. With this awareness, we can move through life changes without losing our composure.

At this point in my life, I know that every transition is different, and no two are alike. Each change has its own unique flavor and set of lessons to learn. Like the movie character Forrest Gump said, "Life was like a box of chocolates . . . you never know what you're gonna get."

# Gallery

Mindful Leadership: Walking the Talk. Speaking at a conference in St. Louis to 350 regional leaders and financial advisors (August 2019/St. Louis, MO).

A Culture of Mindfulness in the Workplace. Presenting to a team of the Federal Reserve Bank of Chicago (September 2018/Chicago, IL).

Mindfulness for Managing Stress and Work–Life Balance. Speaking and guiding a mindfulness workshop for an HR event in New York City (June 2019/Brooklyn, NY).

Mindful Leadership: Developing Self-Awareness. Keynoted at a conference in Denver with leadership from over 50 organizations (December 2019/ Denver, CO).

Mindful Leadership: Walking the Talk for AT&T (July 2022/Dallas, TX).

Mindfulness, Mental Health, and Workplace Culture for the Association of Government Accountants (August 2022/Anaheim, CA).

Mindfulness, Mental Health, and Workplace Culture for the Association of Government Accountants (August 2022/Anaheim, CA).

# Acknowledgments

Just as it takes a village to raise a child, at least for me, a similar idea applies to writing a book. Without the help of my many good friends and well-wishers, I know I couldn't have completed this book.

I'd like to start by thanking Shyamananda Das, a dear mentor, friend, and dedicated monk, who provided just the right amount of inspiration and push to get me to stop procrastinating and complete my book. Without him, this would have remained as an incomplete manuscript on my hard drive.

Govinda Das, a mentor, friend, and big-brother-like figure, has seen me through many stages of my life and has provided me with invaluable emotional support. Without being that pillar in my life, I don't think I would have been able to complete this project. I thank him for his constant encouragement and guidance.

Without the continuous care and professional support of Dr. Ramana Vinjamuri, I could not have brought this project to the final stages of completion. I am so deeply grateful to him and very indebted for his relentless and selfless mood in assisting me with this project. He has assisted with so many aspects of the book that I could write an entire page just praising his contributions.

Many other friends, who I would like to offer heartfelt gratitude to, who have assisted and encouraged me in a variety of ways throughout the process are: Dr. Christopher Fici, Rohan Gupta, Shilpi Lohia, Joseph Caruso, Chintan Raja, and my parents, Govind and Rekha.

# About the Author

**Pandit Dasa** is a mindful leadership expert, author, and motivational keynote speaker. His inspirational speeches aim to create a more mindful workplace culture that increases productivity and improves retention. He encourages leadership and co-workers to appreciate and celebrate the success and contributions of others.

This attitude fosters trust, enhances teamwork, and greatly impacts employee performance. Pandit emphasizes the importance of leading without ego and highlights the importance of cultivating self-awareness and personal growth and development.

Pandit captures the audience's attention by sharing his journey on how and why he spent 15 years living as a monk in New York City, the incredible life and leadership lessons he learned from that experience, and why he's no longer a monk. His story is chronicled in his book *Urban Monk*.

Pandit Dasa has spoken to many Fortune 100 and Fortune 500 companies. Some of the organizations he has spoken to are: Google, NASA, Citibank, IBM, State Farm, Federal Reserve Bank of Chicago, Kellogg's, Cadillac, Whirlpool, Nationwide Insurance, SAP, Bank of America, Morgan Stanley, AMC Theatres, Intel, WeWork, Royal Bank of Canada, AMC Networks, Novartis, Comcast, TD Ameritrade, JPMorgan Chase, The World Bank, World Government Summit, SHRM National Convention, Oracle HCM Convention, and many others.

www.panditdasa.com

# Index

**Q**



**R**